# Bannister
## and
# Beyond

# Bannister and Beyond

## Beyond

### The Mystique of the Four-Minute Mile

## Jim Denison

BREAKAWAY BOOKS
HALCOTTSVILLE, NEW YORK
2003

Bannister and Beyond: The Mystique of the Four-Minute Mile

Copyright 2003 by Jim Denison

ISBN: 1-891369-35-0

Library of Congress Control Number: 2003102249

Published by Breakaway Books

P.O. Box 24

Halcottsville, NY 12438

(800) 548-4348

**www.breakawaybooks.com**

FIRST EDITION

# Contents

To running, which, like art, offers us a treasury of lasting impressions.

## Acknowledgments

While largely a solitary event, writing a book still remains a communal act. Consider, for example, the 21 men who offered me their stories of their first four-minute mile. To me this truly represents a sacred gift, because by sharing his story a man also shares his life. So thank you all for your generosity and kindness. I hope you find that I have represented your experiences with care and respect. To my publisher, Garth Battista, thank you for your encouragement throughout this process. I would also like to thank the dozens of individuals who forwarded email addresses and phone numbers to me so that I could make the necessary contacts to complete my interviews. Certainly the international running community is a large one, but I've also found it to be incredibly warm and open. Finally, to Pirkko, I'm sure you never imagined you'd come to know so much about the four-minute mile. Thank you for listening to me and supporting me as this project took shape. Without your wisdom, my work, like my life, wouldn't be half as satisfying.

# Introduction

The four-minute mile: four laps in four minutes: simple, neat, balanced, clean. A sweep of the track in sync with a sweep of the watch, the four-minute mile is an athletic standard known the world over. Even in today's metric age the challenge of a four-minute mile continues to inspire young runners and excite sport fans everywhere. Indeed, a mile run in less than four minutes is a true test of an athlete's physical and mental capabilities. Unlike the burst of speed needed to cover the dashes, or the methodical sense of pacing required to endure the marathon, success as a miler enlists a sublime combination of speed and stamina, tactics and courage, and patience and spontaneity. The mile's four-lap, four-beat rhythm also ideally suits the human attention span; it's a seductive four-act drama with a clear beginning, middle, and end.

Since records in track and field were first set down in England in 1860, the mile has survived as one of the sport's premier events. Through the late 19th and early 20th centuries great sportsmen across Europe and America sought their fame and fortune as milers—Walter George, Paavo Nurmi, Glenn Cunningham. Bookmakers, too, seized on the public's fascination with the mile and believed as they did with boxing that miling could capture people's emotions and garner a wager.

As the mile world record fell from 4 minutes and 55 seconds in 1861, to 4:18 in 1884, and to 4:12 in 1915, talk quickly turned to the possibility of a mile under four minutes. The English coach Walter Harrington asserted in 1921, "Times are dropping . . . men are strengthening . . . soon no barrier, even four minutes, will hold milers prisoner." The American impresario Asa Bushnell, who organized grand mile invitationals at Princeton University in the early 1930s, believed that packed stadiums, international rivalries, and man's undying curiosity "to see the other side" would quickly bring about a four-minute mile.

The mile's progression has always been a talking point—from the great rivalry between Sebastian Coe and Steve Ovett that saw the world record lowered an astonishing three times in just 18 days in 1981 and reported daily on the front page of the *New York Times,* to banner headlines announcing new mile records in the *London Times* 100 years earlier. And across towns and villages where a four-minute mile has never been run, local promoters attempt to create this spectacle as a way of anointing "their place" a legitimate track-and-field town. Despite the mile's elimination from major championships in favor of the 1500 meters, it remains current and contemporary: Meet organizers include it on their program—Oslo's Dream Mile, Rome's Golden Mile—fans and journalists anticipate faster times yet, and statisticians chart the year's top 50 performances.

The four-minute mile brings to sport a universally appreciated event. What was the lead story of the inaugural issue of *Sports Illustrated?* Coverage of the Miracle Mile from Vancouver, Canada, August 7, 1954, when England's Roger Bannister and Australia's John Landy met for the first time as the world's only sub-four-minute milers. Or consider the attention lavished on Mr. Alan Webb—newspaper and magazine stories, interviews on early-morning and late-night television talk shows—when on January 20, 2001, he became the first American schoolboy since 1967 to run a sub-four-minute mile. He showed us that good times are still on offer, and that past glories and records can be surpassed.

As a point of comparison, where is the history and lore around the 7-foot high jump, or the 13-minute 5000 meters, or for that matter any other barrier in track and field? Why didn't the first man to run under 10 seconds for 100 meters become a household name the way Roger Bannister did when he ran the first four-minute mile? Perhaps it's because the four-sided frame of a four-minute mile, measured and timed in four equal parts, is intuitively grander and in some way more admired. In a similar vein, not every painting in a museum is a Monet or a Michelangelo. Masterpieces do exist; they exist in art, and, as exemplified by the lofty status of the four-minute mile, they obviously exist in sport.

Officially it wasn't until 1933 when the New Zealander, Jack Lovelock, ran 4:07.6 that the term *four-minute mile* was coined by a *New York Herald* sports reporter. In the next 10 years, however, Lovelock's world record fell only 1.6 seconds, prompting leading sports commentators to speculate that there must be some kind of "wall" at four minutes. But then in 1943 Sweden's Arne Andersson produced a stunning 4:02.6, followed the next year by 4:01.6. And later that same year his countryman Gunder Hägg ran

4:01.4. "Surely a breakthrough was near," clamored the sporting press. "Whatever mysteries lay on the other side of four minutes were bound to be discovered."

But the Swedes' progress stalled, and Hägg's record remained intact for 10 long years. This prompted leading scientists, doctors, and coaches to speculate on whether four minutes was humanly possible. Writing recently about this period in sport, Frank Deford of *Sports Illustrated* said, "The poles had been reached, the mouth of the Nile found, the deepest oceans marked, the tallest mountain scaled, and the wildest jungles trekked but the distance of ground that measured a mile continued to resist all efforts to traverse it, on foot, in less than four minutes." Whoever broke four minutes first, therefore, would achieve a heroic feat and establish himself as the boldest explorer of his time. Thus, entering the 1950s 4:00.0 became a symbolic figure, and its quest essential to our mythology.

Roger Bannister's 1955 autobiography, *First Four Minutes,* stands as a testament to the demands of running a four-minute mile. On May 6, 1954, the day Bannister ran history's first sub-four-minute mile on a cold and damp Iffley Road track, Oxford, England, he was 25 years old, 6 feet 1¼ inches tall, and 154 pounds. Bannister was an Oxford University graduate serving his medical internship at St. Mary's Hospital, London. His previous best mile time was four minutes and two seconds—the British record, and equal third on the all-time world list.

On the afternoon of May 6 Bannister arrived at Oxford off the morning train from London. He was nervous and worried as he contemplated the windy, rainy conditions. And he questioned his worthiness to become the First Sub-Four-Minute Miler. Doubts circulated inside his head as he stepped up to the line. And most certainly he heard voices: journalists, coaches, scientists, and all the milers before him who had come close to breaking four minutes but failed. *It can't be done, Roger. It can't be done.* But above all, Bannister was a patriot and determined to run for King and Country and ensure, unlike the ascent of Everest the year before, that if a sub-four-minute mile was to be run, by God, it would be run by an Englishman.

Bannister's quarter-mile intermediate times were perfect—57.4, 1:58.2, 3:00.5—and his statement to the press following his 3:59.4 triumph apt. "I felt suddenly and gloriously free of the burden of athletic ambition that I had been carrying for years. No words could be invented for such supreme happiness, eclipsing all other feelings. I thought at the moment I could never again reach such a climax of single-mindedness."

Since Bannister's epic feat, close to 1,000 men from over 50 countries have broken four minutes for the mile—making it safe to conclude that a four-minute mile isn't an English achievement anymore. It's global, and it has certainly aged well in the 50 years since Bannister gave us the first one. Every year, in fact, runners across the world set out to emulate Bannister's feat and measure themselves against the history he made. And for some their first sub-four is positively transformational, a sporting epiphany that forever alters how they view themselves. While for others it's a crucial bridge to cross before larger goals can be set. Yet in a strange omission of history, few records or statements exist besides Bannister's own literary account in 1955 of how it actually feels to break four minutes for the first time. Our understanding and appreciation of this landmark event has been seemingly cut off post-Bannister. And why should this be when the challenge and prestige of running four minutes survives. This book is intended to address this omission and pick up where Bannister left off.

Collected here, therefore, are in-depth interviews with 21 sub-four-minute milers all speaking about the meaningfulness and significance of breaking four minutes for the first time beginning with the second man to run below four minutes, John Landy. In an attempt to span five decades of the four-minute mile, however, and present a variety of cultures, styles, and abilities, I have deliberately selected a wide array of milers to interview: from those who broke four minutes dozens of times to those who did so only once; from those who were professional milers to those who were strictly amateur; from those who came from countries with no miling tradition to those who were brought up on the mile; and from those who went on to set world records and win Olympic medals to those who remained distinctly sub-elite. Yet despite this vast diversity, every single miler here remarked on one thing: how momentous and memorable his first sub-four was.

It must also be said that these interviews offer more than just an oral record of fifty years of sub-four-minute miles. They are also portraits of 21 very different men—Americans, Europeans, Africans, Australians, New Zealanders. And don't believe for a minute that asking an individual to reflect on a single moment—his first sub-four-minute mile—makes for a superficial or shallow portrait. That can never be the case when exploring, as

I have tried to do, how individuals' experiences and opportunities are bound up in their times. For example, consider the competitive philosophy of Herb Elliott, or the aggression of John Walker, or the guile of Steve Cram, and how differently each of these great milers approached and reacted to his first four-minute mile. Therein lies the advantage of an interview: it provides the opportunity to access an individual's own words and write a story that is unique, informative, and compelling to behold.

In some ways it might seem curious to write a book celebrating "a First Time." After all, our first time doing so many things is often clumsy, messy, or embarrassing. Recall such firsts as riding a bicycle or delivering a speech, to name just two. Typically, practice leads to our latter performances out-stripping the execution, efficiency, and style of our first. As a result, we tend to forget many of our firsts as we pass from novice to expert. In this light, firsts are often adolescent or accidental; they are naive and less pleasurable than a rehearsed, planned replay. But not all firsts necessarily receive low judges' marks, or become fodder for bad memories. Many, like a pitcher's first no-hitter, or a writer's first novel, are extraordinary—a spectacular vision of the future—and require years of hard work, planning, and repeated failures and adjustments.

So it is with an individual's first four-minute mile: No one runs under four minutes for a mile accidentally, or as a beginning runner. No one. Thus, the stories in this book aren't innocent or ignorant firsts—a first kiss, a first fish caught—but the celebration and recognition of a mature first brought about by deliberate experience, dedication, ability, and skill. Four minutes isn't the result of some unconscious biological determinant like a growth spurt. Advancement, graduation, and success in any field must be marked by some public achievement that is widely known and respected. Thanks to Roger Bannister, every miler over the last 50 years has had such a mark. For a runner's first time under four minutes is a fantastic achievement, and the culmination of a life-sustaining story that out of respect for the preciousness of time and the glory of talent should be noted, recorded, and read.

# On the Path to History

## JOHN LANDY
### (Australia)

**First sub-4: June 21, 1954, 3:58.0, Turku, Finland**
**Personal best: 3:58.0**
**Total sub-4s: 5**

*M*elbourne, *the artistic and cultural center of Australia. The National Opera, Ballet, and Symphony all housed in elaborate downtown quarters on the banks of the Yarra River. Once the national capital, and today the state capital of Victoria, Melbourne is a sporting town, too. Formula One, the Australian Open, cricket, Australian-rules football, the Melbourne Cup, the Olympics in '56 . . .*

*I'm walking these streets thinking that I could be somewhere else. Europe perhaps, or the East Coast of America. Definitely an older, more established place; someplace besides this "New World" under the equator. The trolley cars, cobbled streets, and sandstone buildings smack of tradition, ancestry, and protocol. And to approach the governor's mansion on a rise in the center of Fitzroy Park casts a stupendous impression— the symmetry of columns and archways, wide Georgian windows, sweeping views, and regal gardens. But it's also a home. A man's residence. The private address of the governor of Victoria, John Landy, the second man to run under four minutes for a mile.*

*Landy is not a household name. Second past the post in one of sport's greatest events equals more anonymity than fame. Who reached Everest's summit after Hillary? And following Neil Armstrong came who exactly? A lost contest can crush some men's spirits, while others craft satisfactory compensatory tales. Will he have one, I wonder?*

*Out in front of the mansion it's exactly as I expected. A cast-iron bronze gilded gate leads into the driveway, a valet in a suit and tie greets me, and there is a gold-leafed guest book to sign with a black fountain pen. This is followed by a short walk through a high-ceilinged foyer with fresh flowers underneath a crystal chandelier on a square antique table. The governor's office itself is paneled in mahogany; two plush leather chairs fill a small alcove where vibrant views of the front lawn spill inside. The fire crackles; sepia-toned pictures in silver frames rest on the mantel.* Where's Roger Bannister now? *I think quietly to myself. Governor Landy enters the room wearing a smart blue suit. He's tan, fit, and slender. Not an old man; not someone who drowned in the wake of his rival. Immediately he welcomes me to Australia, and soon thereafter we begin.*

When you were running the mile, Governor, in the early 1950s, was there a sense that the four-minute mile was some sort of Everest that needed to be conquered?

The quest to run a four-minute mile did have clear parallels with the quest to climb Mount Everest. People wondered whether it was the limit of human capability—could anyone possibly run a mile that fast? This was reinforced by the fact that over a period of about 10 years many great runners had come fairly close to breaking four minutes, but were unable to reach that summit, so to speak. The Swedes, Arne Andersson and Gunder Hägg, as I'm sure you know, came very close.

Sure, they both ran 4:01 in 1944.

But really the four-minute mile has even deeper origins, going back to the great Finnish runner of the 1920s, Paavo Nurmi, who ran 4:10, and in the 1930s the rivalry between Glenn Cunningham of America and Jack Lovelock from New Zealand. They both ran close to 4:05, and from their diaries we know that they entertained the possibility of breaking four minutes. Do you know that there were rumors that they might have actually done it?

Didn't Cunningham claim to have done it alone in practice, and weren't there two British doctors who said they timed Lovelock over a mile at Motspur Park in London in 3:52?

That's right. But of course we don't know about the accuracy of those tracks, or whether their watches were working correctly. Regardless, the idea was at least being considered, and this was all prewar. So in total, the four-minute mile had a run of about 18 years as a standard that man couldn't seem to reach.

No wonder there was so much mystique surrounding it. Do you think without the war things might have been different?

Who could seriously think about running during the war . . . only the Swedes who were neutral. Even here in Australia resources were scarce to train athletes. It could have only been more severe in Europe and America. In fact, there was hardly any information at all in those days to follow developments in running. I can't remember ever reading articles in the newspaper, or seeing results, or coming across any type of training advice. Mind you, maybe that was just Australia.

How did you develop your training program?

By myself, mainly, and from observing others, particularly the Europeans when I was in Helsinki for the 1952 Olympic Games. Watching and meeting Emil Zatopeck [triple gold medalist in 1952 from Czechoslovakia] had the biggest influence on me. He was incredibly generous and willing to talk about his training. So I spent a lot of time learning from him. For example, he showed me how to carry my arms more like a distance runner. At that time in Australia we used to drop our arms low, down by our hips; there was also the idea that we couldn't let our heels touch the ground, so we had to use these flat sprinting shoes with no support in the backs. That was something I changed straightaway when I got back from Helsinki. I began holding my arms higher and letting my whole foot roll and push off the ground. Immediately I felt more balanced and relaxed; I was using less energy, too.

And of course, I learned from Zatopeck about his famous repetition training on the track, doing one lap then another with a short rest in between, and using accurate timing and careful record keeping. I applied all of these ideas to myself and devised a program to follow.

You had no coach to help you?

No. I ran alone at night on a gravel track after I got home from work. I'd begin by jogging a few laps, then I'd do some various repetitions, and I'd finish by doing a few sprints.

What about long runs on the roads?—or was your training entirely track-based?

It was largely track-based. Lots and lots of repetitions. Only a few long runs. I can say now that it was quite boring. But I realized that I had wasted my time traveling all the way to Finland so underprepared. I was determined after running so badly there—I was eliminated in the first round of the 1500 meters—that in the future I would make my best effort.

So after the '52 games you came back to Australia with renewed determination . . .

I trained like the dickens for three months—September, October, November—to prepare for our summer season. I had that advantage as a Southern Hemisphere athlete, I didn't have to wait a whole year to make amends for Helsinki. I think the greatest mile race I ever ran came after this period of very serious training.

December 13, 1952.

That's right. I improved to 4:02 from 4:11. It came so easily, very easily. I had no idea I had gotten myself into such good shape; that result was completely unexpected, and on a chewed-up old track. In fact, there is a famous story behind that race which might explain why I ran so well. I was delayed getting to the meeting because on the way I passed through a little town that had the most beautiful chocolate nut sundaes. Well, I had to have one even though I was racing in a hour. You see, I was quite relaxed about the whole day, and the sundae was gorgeous.

That time would have catapulted you to the forefront of the worldwide race to break four minutes.

It did, and many people questioned it. The Americans in particular were skeptical. They thought something must have been funny with the track or the timing for me to have improved by so much. They knew, too, that I had the good Australian weather coming and a summer of racing ahead of me. I'm sure they were nervous that I might get under four before their own boys, who were stuck in winter. I was actually asked to run again two weeks later to prove myself; a reporter from the *New York Times* came all the way out here to watch the race and verify it. That was a hot and windy day, not ideal conditions, but I ran 4:02.8, anyway. The reporter went home satisfied.

Were you generally a relaxed runner?

I wouldn't say that. I ran on a lot of nervous energy. Bannister was the same, you know. And Lovelock, he was famous for his sleepless nights before races. But I do think I became more of an intuitive runner as my career went on. In 1953, for example, I recorded and timed everything I did. I was like a bookkeeper with my training diary. But beginning in 1956, I was much more natural and easygoing. I stepped away from the track and started running on the beach or through the forest. I think those were my best running years.

What do you mean *best?*

The most enjoyable . . . the easiest.

But you never ran a mile as fast as you did in 1954, under that "boring" repetition training program.

That's true, but I think I matured as a person in the later years of my career. And that's sometimes as important as fast times.

Did you ever see yourself as a discoverer or bold adventurer when you were pursuing the first four-minute mile?

I suppose my aims in athletics were twofold. I wanted to win an Olympic gold medal—obviously I never did [Landy won a Bronze Medal in the 1956 Olympic 1500]—and I wanted to set the mile world record, which I did do. The four-minute mile never appealed to me terribly much. I know that's easy to say now because I didn't do it first, but to me it seemed too contrived, just a round figure that conveniently popped up in front of the world record. And for some reason, quite a few people seemed to bounce off it as they figured out how to lower the existing world record. This then drew the public in, because what you had now was this simple round figure that the average sport fan could identity with, four minutes. For example, had I run 3:41 for 1500 meters, which is just as good as a four-minute mile, no one would have cared. People would have said, *So what.* What I'm saying is that there was a lot of coincidence and nonsense in it. It was just a round figure that created loads of hype. But its image among the public was tremendous, there's no denying that. It practically became this romantic quest, because like I said to you earlier, if you go back to Nurmi and Lovelock and the others before Bannister and me, this four-minute problem had been around a long time. To be quite honest, I'm still surprised it took until 1954 for someone to run under four minutes, particularly as I was so close to doing it myself quite early on.

That's certainly true; you ran 4:02 five times and 4:01 two times between December 1952 and April 1954, all before Bannister's big day. What did you think it would take to get on the other side of four minutes?

I really felt that all I needed to do was run on a better track. I believed that I was training my hardest and racing as hard as I could, but the tracks here were shocking. They had holes and divots and were uneven. Also, I would have been just as happy to have simply gotten under Hägg's record by a little bit. Then after that, start thinking about running faster and maybe breaking four minutes. So it did frustrate me that I couldn't even get past the old record, even by just a tenth of a second. But it was the bad tracks largely. Again, I knew I had to be able to get close to 4:01 and break the record, which was what I thought was likely to happen. I thought the same of

Bannister and Wes Santee, the top American miler at the time. I was surprised, really, that the record went under four all in one effort. I thought the three of us would inch it down. For example, I never thought I'd go from 4:01 all the way to 3:58 in one race. I never envisioned that at all. And particularly so soon after Bannister's race.

Just six weeks . . .

Right, six weeks later and we have another mile world record and the second runner under four minutes when it had taken practically 18 years for the first man to do it.

So why the sudden improvements?

Speaking for myself, there were two reasons. Like I've been saying, a better track. The track in Turku was lovely. The Finns really did a great job in preparing it. And secondly, the competition that Chris Chataway provided helped tremendously. At the bell, with one lap to go, he was right on me. He was a powerful runner and I could hear him breathing behind me. Having him there so close was a great stimulus. I never had that in Australia. So putting it all together, I made that great improvement, ran my maiden sub-four, and set a new world record.

What led you to travel to Finland—why Turku?

I needed races; it was April 1954, the Australian winter was coming, I knew I was in great shape, and I was determined to give that world record a crack. Also, 1954 was the year of the Empire Games. They were to be held in Vancouver in August, so I needed to start making my way over to America and Europe anyway. And everywhere I went in Europe there were mile races. I ran a mile in Stockholm and another one in Helsinki before my Turku race. But Turku, of course, is a fabulous running city, being the home of Paavo Nurmi. The people there wanted to see a mile, and their support was fantastic. I was so glad that I could set a new world record for them.

So if there were mile races all over Europe, and the people in Turku really wanted to see a sub-four-minute mile, maybe it wasn't just a convenient barrier? Perhaps there was something intuitively appealing about the mile? For example, interest in other round barriers like the 7-foot high jump or the 10-second 100 meters haven't been sustained to the degree that a four-minute mile has.

Well, it was clearly a popular event throughout the world. More people did it, for one thing. A person could always go out and run a mile, and therefore people related to us racing a mile. There's something to do with the evenness, too. There's that symmetry, four laps, like a play in four acts. And the balance of speed and endurance that it takes to run a good mile is also special. It's a real marriage of those two qualities, much more so than any other event. That's partly why it's interesting to watch a mile. In the same event you might have someone who's speed-oriented and someone who's endurance-oriented. How are they going to offset each other's strengths and weaknesses? Like when I raced Bannister in Vancouver at the Empire Games. He was a real kicker and I was a front runner. I knew I needed to extinguish that kick of his. A slow pace, that was his caper, so my hand was forced. I had to set a fast pace—otherwise I had no chance of beating him. And I almost did. If I could have just stretched the lead out another few yards I might have been able to hold him off. But you see, that's exciting. No other event can bring together runners with completely opposite styles. Everyone who runs the 100 is fast. Everyone in the marathon has tremendous stamina. Where's the interest? What's contributing to varied tactics being employed if everyone has the same strengths and weaknesses? But that's not the case with the mile.

Now, the 1500 meters, that's not a race at all. What a shame that we're stuck with the 1500. It's a tragedy. It's awful. There's nothing graceful about it. You don't start where you finish, it's ugly, it has no elegance. I know some people will call me old-fashioned for thinking this way, but the mile is a vastly better race. Split times are impossible to follow in a 1500. As a runner you can never develop any rhythm, either. At the minimum we should be running the 1600. That would at least be four laps. But three and three-quarter laps? That really bothers me. Nobody on the street can tell you a good 1500 time, but the mile they can. It's not nonsense I'm speaking, there's a real difference between the 1500 and the mile. Like I said, the mile is better. I prefer it anyway. And when I was running I think the crowds drew a deeper meaning from the mile, certainly compared to the other events. Perhaps they didn't quite recognize it themselves, or maybe it was just something they felt, but I think that "feeling" drew them to the mile. It has an intuitive appeal, the mile; a real natural interest. Whereas what draws people to a 1500? Nothing. So, yes, the mile is special. In making me think about it, perhaps what I said earlier was a bit flippant. For instance, there is this balance to the number four in and of itself, more so than the number three. And four's just the right number of laps. With the 800, two laps is too few to get involved, and for races that go beyond a mile people tune out after five, six, seven laps. They lose interest. It's not so emotional. Like a boring play. But that number four is the perfect attention grabber. These subtle things remain unconscious in most spectators, but they do affect us. It's architectural, too, the mile. Like the way a building is put together. We like buildings that are symmetrical: four columns, two on each side. The same number of windows back and front. That's the four-minute mile, everything's even and balanced and in order. So it's no wonder, really, that it was so popular.

Governor, for me, looking fondly or perhaps longingly at the early 1950s, when running seemed to be so much more appreciated as a sport than it is today, I imagine the quest to run under four minutes first, with you here in Australia, Bannister in England, and Santee in America, resembling something like the space race or the race to discover the structure of DNA. Was it like that? Did the stakes ever feel that high to you?

I feel very strongly that I was just fortunate to be a person running the mile at a stage when there was all this interest. Now, mind you I encouraged a lot of that interest because of my many efforts in coming so close to four minutes and bouncing off it, which propelled me into this position at the forefront of this race or chase or whatever you want to call it. But my view of that is that it was chance. I was just around at that time. I was a good runner born at the right time and with enough ability to attain a high profile and participate in one of the most exciting moments in the history of our sport. For example, had I been born earlier I would have been the same runner with the same potential but I know I wouldn't have run as fast because the interest, hype, and excitement that pushed me forward wouldn't have been so pervasive. So in a sense I was lucky, a product of my times, and that situation enabled me to run faster and develop myself further than if I had been part of an another era of miling. I guess timing is everything in terms of who acquires attention and who doesn't. If I had been born later and carried with me the same abilities, I never would have had as big a profile. I was a competent runner racing at a time when everyone's attention was focused on this goal—breaking four minutes—and I happened to have enough talent to become involved in this period. So over time, as I've gotten older, I've come to accept more and more that my legacy in athletics is really just an accident presented by a lucky opportunity.

Was there respect for breaking four minutes for the first time honorably, or in a gentlemanly fashion—that is, in a legitimate race? In other words, no obvious setups.

I wouldn't have done it that way myself, using a pacesetter. I didn't want any part of something questionable, which was how pacesetting was seen at that time. Although if someone else did it with a pacesetter and lots of other advantages it wouldn't have upset me. But I wanted to do it on my own. I wanted to lead. I wanted to control the race. That was my belief. I can see now that I made myself too vulnerable by doing that, by being prominent in my races. I could have been a much better tactical runner; I did expend a lot of energy running from the front. But my interest as an athlete was running fast times, and in Australia I couldn't wait around for someone to help me. I had to go out and do it myself. Also, pacing wasn't allowed here. A paced record would have been queried and probably less respected. But don't take that to mean that I have any problem with Bannister's run, and the assistance he received from Brasher and Chataway. In every way it was a fantastic performance.

That's very much an Australian sensibility, isn't it . . . individual achievement, ingenuity, getting the job done yourself.

It was essential at one period in our history. Who's going to wait six months for a part they need to fix their tractor to arrive all the way from England? Figure out a way to fix it. Likewise, with such wide expanses of land and so few people, if you want to run a world record, go and do it. You can't wait around for someone else to help you. And that's the type of person I was; I think that's reflected in my style and tactics as a miler: Lead, go for it.

Did being Australian influence your determination to get under four minutes first as a way of showing up the British? I mean, do you think it was important for Australians, and subsequently Australian national identity, to follow your progress and cheer you on?

Certainly people were interested in this thing because we had a contender. And the crowds reflected that. After my early 4:02 in December, 1952 great numbers of people started to come see me run. Sometimes there were as many as 20,000 or 30,000 at these informal twilight meetings. The crowds were swarmed all over the place. The anticipation from people was very high. And that was hard for me because sometimes I knew the record wasn't going to fall. For example, the wind might have been too much. But you still have to try.

What did the wind do to you?

Rhythm was important to me. I liked my pace to feel even, and with wind it's uneven. Upwind . . . downwind. That disturbed me. There is too much strain, no smooth, gliding, effortless stride. As I know too well, good performances come when things feel easy.

What were your thoughts when you found out Bannister had done it?

I wasn't going to go and shoot myself if that's what you think. Certainly not. My first thoughts were, *Fantastic . . . good on him.* But it certainly convinced me that I could do it, too. I mean, we had been running neck and neck. But a lot of people assumed that once Bannister had done it he removed this giant psychological barrier. But I don't believe that at all. Because if that was true I would have been cognizant of how fast I was running in Finland, and whether I was approaching four minutes. But like all my races, I was just trying to win and the sub-four simply fell out of it. I had no idea that I was running world-record pace. I only heard the three-lap time, and it was inside three minutes, but I had been inside three minutes before and then faded so I wasn't thinking this or that, only *Hold off Chataway*. But people wouldn't stop insisting that I ran that time because the barrier was gone. In other words, all thanks to Bannister. But honestly, an important reason why more of us started to get under four minutes was because we got to an advanced level of fitness. That's not to take anything away from Bannister's race. It was a phenomenal race and run under very difficult weather conditions. But as athletes we were blind back then, trying one thing then another. And some things we were getting better at. But we didn't understand how to mix speed and slow work, or recovery. Today training is more purposeful and predictable. What we did was so amateurish compared to what they do today. The gymnastic work they do was nothing we had heard of. Quite simply, they know better today what's required to run a fast mile so it takes away a lot of the guesswork.

Do you ever get drawn into nostalgic musings of being in great shape and on top of your game like you were 47 years ago?

Well, I can't run anymore because of some pains in my legs, and as a result I don't find myself breathing heavily or rhythmically for any sustained periods, which was what really brought on all the feelings and sensations of running and being fit for me. It was the deep breathing that gave me a joy of movement and made me feel strong and fluid. I loved that. But running was what I did as a young man. I tend not to look back at things too much, or read too heavily into what was then and what's now. The fact is, I can't run anymore and that just has to be fine.

What do you make of today's mile world record?

To be quite honest, 3:43 doesn't really amaze me. They have better training, tracks, race conditions, and a more diverse pool of athletes. I never ran against any Africans, but had you asked me back in 1954 if I thought someone would run 3:43 one day I would have said no way whatsoever. Impossible. My God, it was hard enough getting under four.

Photo by Central Press

# A Northern Man

## DEREK IBBOTSON
### (United Kingdom)

**First sub-4: August 6, 1956, 3:59.4, London**
**Personal best: 3:57.2**
**Total Sub-4s: 4**

*Y*orkshire, *in northern England, is where Derek Ibbotson, the former mile world-record holder and the ninth man to run a sub-four-minute mile, grew up running and now lives in retirement. I arrive in Huddersfield off the morning train from London, and immediately the station's architecture strikes me. It's prescient, really, this 1879 Georgian structure, such a testament to symmetry and order, in the birthplace of a great four-minute-miler.*

*On each side of the two-story entranceway to the station there is a row of four columns flanked by an additional single-story open pavilion. Here they are in concert, two sets of four: four structures, four columns . . . four laps, four minutes.*

*Standing beside his car in the open plaza that frames the station, Derek welcomes me to Yorkshire and then quickly points to the station. "The stone's local . . . Yorkshire stone, straight from the ground in those foothills behind you. She's grand, this building. Even as a lad it was my favorite."*

*"I'm not surprised, Derek," I say. And we drive off down the road for lunch and a chat.*

Derek, where were you the day Bannister broke the four-minute mile?

I was in the pub. We had no telly at home, and so I watched the race there. It was obvious to me that Roger would be the one to do it because Oxford had the best coach in Franz Stampfl. I had been following all the lads' progress: Landy, Santee, Chataway, Bannister. But no one else had advantages like Bannister and Chataway. Training was seat-of-the-pants stuff back then. The boys who worked with Stampfl, I believe, really benefited.

Could Chataway have been first under four minutes?

Possibly, but from what I've heard Stampfl figured that Roger had the speed. Chataway was really a three miler. Stampfl believed the mile was a speed event, and he geared Roger up for months convincing him he could do it. All credit to Stampfl, you know. He decided everything about the first four-minute mile: who would be in the race, the date, what time it would start. In fact, the wind was so strong that day that he kept delaying the start. Finally, when the flag on the church across the street dipped below horizontal, he quickly got things under way.

What was the atmosphere like in the pub where you watched the race?

Remember, this was groundbreaking stuff. Everyone knew about the four-minute mile. So people were tense; they were very quiet during the race. And the pace was looking good—58, 1:59 . . . And Bannister looked steady, too. Then a bloody ruckus broke out when the result was announced. It was good that an Englishman did it first. We needed something positive back then.

Why do you think people like to watch a mile race?

As a spectator the mile is something you can get your teeth into. And the four-minute mile is this clear barrier: Four laps . . . four minutes. Now take your 400, just the one lap—and with the stagger, who can follow that? The mile is pure drama that unfolds before you. Or a 6-mile race, so boring. Attracting support means keeping people's interest; with a mile race something exciting can happen every lap.

Why do you think it took so long for someone to break four minutes?

I don't think they believed it could be done, as simple as that. The record stood at 4:01 for so long, and because of the war there was no sport for seven years. It wasn't until 1948, when they revitalized the Olympics in London, that men resumed running. The world was starting up again, wasn't it? Previously everything had gone into the war effort. But suddenly people wanted something positive to think about, and this four-minute thing got plenty of folks excited.

Did the hype around the first four-minute mile motivate you to become a runner?

I was already a runner. I had been as a boy. You saw our beautiful fields and countryside 'round here. For a lad with loads of energy and friends scattered about, I simply ran everywhere.

Like the Kenyans today.

Exactly like that.

When did you start competing?

I probably never would have run a race if it wasn't for my older brother. He was a champion footballer [soccer] and cricketer, and I knew I would never be better than him, which meant I had to find another sport, because more than anything I wanted to top him. Then in grammar school they held a cross-country race and I waltzed through it. And that was that.

Did you enjoy winning races?

Well, I'll tell you this. When I was 16 I won the Yorkshire Junior Mile Championship. That was my first proper title. This was on a Saturday, and the next day we had our big Sunday lunch. Now in those days—this was 1948—we had Yorkshire pudding with onions and gravy to start. And as meat was still being rationed, you'd eat as much pudding as possible to fill up before the meat dish, which was always very small. So then, the Yorkshire pudding would come out of the oven in a square tin and my Dad would take it and cut it into sections. First he'd cut half for himself, then he'd cut a quarter for me mum, and finally my brother and I would share the remaining quarter. But on the Sunday after I won my Yorkshire mile title, he took the square tin and cut it in half as usual, then like he always did cut the remaining half in half. But instead of taking the half for himself, he put it on my plate and said, "This is to congratulate you, son, on becoming a Yorkshire champion." That was it. And I never got another half of Yorkshire pudding again. So you see, dads were powerful figures in those days. Their respect and influence meant everything. My dad was hardworking and strict. I never questioned him. One Saturday I was playing in a football match and he said to me afterward, "Son, you've got lots of energy but not much of an idea of the game. I'd say you'd be better off sticking to running." And that was that, I became a runner.

You mentioned rations just before. What effect did the war have on your running?

I was just a wee lad in 1940, but in one way the war did play a part in my athletic development. You see, the town across the way had a fireworks company, Standard Fireworks, the biggest fireworks manufacturer in Britain. But during the war they made flares for lost pilots to signal their position in the Channel or wherever. And obviously they wanted these flares to stay in the air for as long as possible to give a search party a greater chance of seeing the signal, so they tested them 'round the clock. Now, attached to each flare was a small square nylon parachute, and because materials and fabrics were scarce during the war, my friends and I would chase after these parachutes for miles and then sell them so they could be made into handkerchiefs and pillowcases or whatever else. And so I have to think all that running around picking up parachutes had an effect on my running ability.

Did the company know you were stealing their parachutes?

What could they do? Those parachutes were landing miles apart, and miles from the factory, all depending on the wind, you see. They couldn't collect them, so why not us? Besides, the extra bob or two in our pockets kept us out of trouble.

So at what point did you begin to train more systematically?

When I joined the RAF in 1954, at 22.

Did you have a coach then?

No, no. Coaches were only for the Oxford and Cambridge boys. Who was going to look after my training, a scruffy northern lad? There was time reserved every afternoon for sport. That was the first time I really began to train seriously and I put together my own program.

How did you know what to do?

I talked and listened and watched just about anything that had to do with running. Which I can tell you wasn't much. We had *Athletics Weekly,* and I read that like the bible, but it was probably Gordon Pirie [the English distance running legend of the late 1940s] who helped me the most. I'd ring Gordon to find out what I should be doing. He'd give me some ideas and between us we worked out different schedules. Although we didn't know how to mix speed work and strength work; we never knew if we were doing too much or not enough. But we had other worries, too, like work and making a living. We were just fitting running into our lives and getting out for a session in the hour or two at night we had available.

Was there a division in British athletics between the Oxbridge group and everyone else?

God, yes. There was a real north-south divide. They had the privileges: coaches, tracks, physical therapy. We had nothing.

Did that cause much resentment?

When it came to selections it did. But you see, I was never too fussed about fancy facilities and whatnot. I had these hills and fields for running; nothing was better than that. And I had confidence in myself and the decisions I was making. Who needed a coach? Running never seemed all that difficult to me. You trained hard, had a laugh, and when it came to racing you went out and took care of business. How's a coach going to help with that? But come selection time for the Olympics and other events, the Oxford favoritism upset me; well . . . Brasher and Chataway at least were always getting advantages, like better travel conditions. The major fixtures were always in London, too, and it was less expensive to bring in a southern runner even if he was slower than a northern runner. They didn't need housing or train fare now, did they? Also, the British Olympic captain always had to come from Oxford. I should have run the 1500 meters at the Melbourne Olympics in 1956, you see. I had the best time for a mile in Britain, but wouldn't you know they selected an Oxford runner, Ian Boyd, because it had already been decided that he would be the British captain. Just bloody rubbish that was.

So you ran the 5K instead . . .

I won a bronze medal. But just the idea that running for Oxford meant different rules applied pissed me off.

Do you think you could have managed a 5K/1500 double in '56?

I think so. There was a full day's rest between events. And the way the race went, fast then slow, I could have won the gold medal with my finishing kick.

With all your success in the 3-mile, when did you begin to consider yourself a miler?

In one way it was an accident. Now, mind you, I used to run a fair few miles, and I was fine at it, producing a 4:04 or a 4:07 without much fuss. Still I wouldn't have called myself a miler. But on August 4 [1956] I ran a 3-mile in a Britain versus Czechoslovakia match and I won in a new British record, and that was a Saturday and two days later on the Monday, which was a Bank

Holiday, there was a meeting in London and they were holding a mile. Ken Finding, who worked for *News of the World,* the outfit that sponsored British athletics, asked me to have a crack at the mile. I really didn't want to. I was tired from the 3-mile, and my wife's cousin from America was arriving on Sunday to spend time with us up in Yorkshire. But you see, in those days they always laid on dinners and dances after the big meetings in London, usually at the Dorchester Hotel. These were quite big dos. So I told Ken if he could get me another ticket for the dance for my wife's cousin I'd run. And he did. Well then, I was running, wasn't I? And it's that race I ran 3:59.4, my first sub-four-minute mile, and began thinking that I could have some decent success as a miler.

Before that was breaking four minutes a goal for you?

Not really, but let me tell you why. I liked to plan my races down to the finest detail: the pace, the competition, the time I was shooting for. Now, most of my energy went into planning 3-mile races. I never actually sat down and planned a fast mile. But that 3:59.4 just came out of the blue.

What impact did that have on your career?

I had another string to my bow now: I could run the mile or the 3-mile. Being a sub-four-minute miler put me in a whole other category of runner. I had my pick of races, and the mile was a damn sight easier than the 3-mile. Hell, I would have been a sprinter if I could have been. But no, I was glad to be seen as a miler. It had so much more prestige than the 3-mile. I loved racing, you see, and I could run more mile races in a season than I could 3-mile races.

What did you love about racing?

Training was boring and racing wasn't. As simple as that, really.

Going back to your first sub-four, was there a point in that race where you thought, *I can break four minutes here?*

In those days, and it's probably still true today, anyone who could run near 4:05 was thinking about four minutes. It was big stuff; it affected every middle-distance runner. After three laps I knew I was close: I was feeling good when the timekeeper shouted, "Three minutes." Usually I don't hear much during my races, but coming into that third lap I was listening for the time.

And your last lap?

It was always my strongest part seeing as I had such a cross-country background. On the backstretch, then, I felt fairly confident that I'd get under. And again I heard someone along the railing yell to me that I could break four minutes. So I just kept running as hard as I could.

What was your reaction when you found out you had done it?

To begin with, I had to wait five minutes for the result. Instead of reporting the time straightaway the announcer went on about it being a track record, a meet record, a British All-Comers record. And I'm in the infield listening to him rabbiting on, waiting for the official time. Mind you, once he said I had equaled the British record I knew. And I had a wee laugh, 3:59.4, exactly what Bannister had done up in Oxford two years earlier. *Funny that,* I thought, *Roger and me sharing the British mile record.*

And the dinner and dance at the Dorchester?

Oh, it was a big night out.

Do you think the unplanned nature of your first sub-four made it more special?

Somewhat. But I planned my mile world record the next year in '57, and that's still very special to me.

What exactly did you plan?

I sat down with Terry O'Connell, who worked for the *Evening News,* and organized the meeting. We decided the field, the pacesetter, and the pace. Most importantly, I wanted Ron Delany in the race because he was the Olympic 1500-meter champion from the year before. I wanted Stanislav Jungwirth because he had just set a new 1500-meter world record. But the plan didn't go so well. The bloke who set the pace had just gotten back from a two-week holiday with his fiancée and hadn't been doing any training. His timing was all off; he went through the first lap in 54 and then 1:55 at 800. This was an unheard-of pace back then. But I knew that Delany had to be hurting as much as me so I hung in there and on the fourth lap, with 300 yards to go, I recovered a bit and took off. And that was that. A new mile world record.

You didn't consider giving up after the pacing had been bungled?

I really thought I could get that record. You see, a month earlier I had come close; I was determined to try again. Now, that was a special race. I was up north and relaxing in my hotel room beforehand when my wife rang to say that she had just given birth to our first daughter. You might imagine I was delighted, and I said to her, "I'm going to go out and break the mile world record today." I ran 3:58.4 and missed by a few tenths. That was a hot day and the pacesetter dropped out early so I was on my own most of the way, which just made it too hard. Otherwise, I think I would have done it. Fancy that as a birthday present for my little girl?

How does it feel to lose a world record?

Funny that, because Herb Elliott, who broke my mile world record, was staying with me before he left to go up to Dublin, where that race was held. Obviously, I had read in the paper that he had broken my record, and a few days later when he was on his way back and I saw his taxi coming up the road I rushed upstairs and piled all his things into his case and put it outside the door. Well there's ol' Herbie knocking on the door and I yell, "Yeah, what the hell do you want?" And he says, "What's my case doing out here?" And I said, "If you think you're staying here after taking my record you can piss off." Then we went out to the pub and toasted his brilliant run.

Derek, did you obey the amateur code as was expected of all runners in your era?

I had to. There was a race in South Africa I was invited to run but couldn't because they couldn't find a manager to go with me.

What do you mean?

According to British Athletics Association rules, a manager had to accompany you on all trips to make sure you weren't being paid.

So you were an amateur, then?

Well, nobody was an amateur, except for maybe Bannister. Now, he didn't need the money, did he? Besides, I don't think Roger liked racing very much so he was never taking time off to run. But every race I ran I always asked for something, and usually the meet organizer would say to me, "What do you want?" Well, maybe we needed a new vacuum cleaner so I'd say that. Or if we needed a dinner service he'd get me that. Quite often the day before a race they'd take me to a wholesale warehouse to pick out my prize before I actually ran. Or I'd get generous expenses, or an added night in the hotel to stay with my wife.

Or an extra ticket to a dance.

Exactly, things like that.

While those are nice prizes, Derek, they're nothing like the millions top milers make today.

They can have their bloody money. We had fun. There was a race we ran in Finland where before the meeting we went to the local hospital to see the matron to tell her there was going to be a dinner with a big meal laid on and a dance and could we invite her girls. So there you have it, 30 Finnish nurses came to our party and we had a fantastic time. Today, that's gone. Guys are grabbing their money, going back to their hotels, then flying out the next day. Plus for us the travel was exciting, not like today where everyone is jumping on a plane. We got to go places most people couldn't: Hungary, Russia, Australia. You really felt honored and special to be a good runner in those days. I wouldn't trade that for anything.

# A Question of Time

## DON BOWDEN
### (United States)

**First sub-4: June 1, 1957, 3:58.7, Stockton, California**
**Personal best: 3:58.7**
**Total Sub-4s: 1**

*W̲ho was the first American to run a sub-four-minute mile?" asked my high school track coach one late spring afternoon 25 years ago. My teammates and I all knew the name, Roger Bannister, the world's first sub-four-minute miler. But the first American?*

*Our coach, gray-haired and track-worn, was a repository of running facts. He smiled as we struggled to provide the correct answer; his broad, unyielding stance across lanes one and two all the time complemented his intellectual advantage.*

*A senior on the team answered, "Wes Santee"—a name I had never heard before.*

*"No," our coach said.*

*"Jim Ryun," Eddie Haggerty said next.*

*"Not him," came the response.*

*Then a hint: "It happened exactly 20 years ago today: June 1, 1957, in Stockton, California." No one said a word.*

*To a 13 year old boy 20 years ago can seem like a lost age. Did they have proper running tracks back then? What kind of sneakers did they wear? But maturing closes gaps, turning differences into interesting talking points. So I know now that runners from the '50s also worried about winning and losing; they got injured, but healed; they formed rivalries that grew into friendships; and they were proud and exhilarated when their stride widened and they took to the air. How do I know all this? A man who made history as the first American to run a sub-four-minute mile told me. Who is this man? The answer is: Don Bowden.*

Don, do you remember how you first heard the news about Roger Bannister breaking the four-minute mile?

Oh, I sure do. That was my senior year of high school, 1954, and I read about it in the newspaper. I was really excited. I mean, what a great achievement. I was also impressed with Bannister's coach, Franz Stampfl. He seemed to be the key figure behind it all. And through that race he demonstrated how a sensible approach to training could lead to huge breakthroughs. I believe he and Bannister changed running forever that day because they showed that four minutes wasn't something to be afraid of.

What exactly scared people about four minutes?

Well, no one knew for sure what was waiting for them on the other side. Was something good or something bad going to occur? It was considered an extreme, after all, like deep-sea diving or going into space. And remember, this barrier had been around for years and years. But why couldn't anyone get past it? It was a real mystery. So when Bannister didn't collapse or have a heart attack after crossing the line everyone was relieved. But that still didn't stop my mother from bringing me to a heart specialist my senior year of high school to make sure all the running I was doing wasn't damaging me, or from writing a letter to my college coach, Brutus Hamilton, the next year asking him if this mile business was any good for her little boy.

And was he able to reassure her?

Yes, she soon found out that her little boy was in good hands. After all,

Brutus thought the true purpose of sport was to build character. He believed that sport should only form part of your life, not your whole life. And he insisted that his athletes develop themselves all around. He never would have endangered one of his runners for the sake of winning or setting a new record. That just wasn't how he thought. He advocated true mind-body integration, like the ancient Greeks. And athletics, to him, was part of the educational process. For example, at Cal we never trained for more than one or two hours a day because Brutus wanted us to have time and energy for other pursuits, particularly our schoolwork. Because back then there was no future in running. Basically, you ran your last race in college and then went and got a job.

It sounds like you had a very special relationship with Brutus.

I always appreciated Brutus's wisdom on and off the track. He was a great coach with a keen intellect and strong character. And I believe I lead a better life today because of his influence. Brutus prepared us for life, not just a single race.

Don, going back to an earlier point you made, would you say that the first sub-four was actually a coaching problem that Stampfl solved, not a psychological barrier that Bannister overcame?

I think getting the first man under four minutes was a combination of things. Obviously, proper training was important to bring the athlete to that point of physical readiness. And Stampfl clearly came up with some innovations in that respect. Like his use of interval training, and strict pacing. But the will of Bannister was extremely important, too. He needed to develop the drive to push his body when he knew it was going to hurt.

Do you think anyone else besides Bannister could have broken four minutes first?

Obviously, there were others who were close, and clearly it would have been done sooner or later by someone, but I do think Bannister was special. He had it in him to achieve this event more than anyone else. He was a man destined for greatness. A true sportsman trying to achieve a supreme goal.

And in the end it became a case of mind over matter. He must have really believed that breaking that barrier was possible. For me, there's no other way to explain how he did it.

What about the American threat to four minutes—was there a sense throughout the United States that running the first four-minute mile was something an American needed to achieve?

There really wasn't any kind of rivalry between nations that surrounded the four-minute mile. At least I never picked up on that. Sure there was competition to do it first, but it was more like this important world sport goal that everyone wanted to see achieved, so the support for anyone close to four minutes was tremendous. People weren't thinking about it in the same way they were the space race or the Cold War. I have to say, I always found the international track community extremely friendly; everyone was on the side of each other, with every individual simply trying to do his best. Overall, I'd say the feeling throughout America when Bannister did it was, *Great, it's been done*. Not, *Why couldn't an American have done it first?*

But surely Americans must have been hoping that Wes Santee would've gotten there first, particularly after he ran 4:02.4 in 1953, almost a year ahead of Bannister's performance?

You're right in saying that people were excited about Wes, including myself. I was actually at the race you just mentioned. It was the Compton Invitational here in California. And I thought Wes would definitely be the first man to get under four minutes. He was such a strong runner. For instance, he ran 55 seconds for his third lap that day, and this was when mid-races surges like that were unheard of. But unfortunately things never worked out for Wes. I saw him the next year at the Compton Invitational, too, when he ran 4:00.6. That was June 1954, and Bannister had already broken four, although an American hadn't. And I thought nothing would stop Wes from doing it first. But amazingly, he couldn't get past that barrier. Six days later, in fact, he ran 4:00.7, and a week after that, 4:00.5. So by the end of 1954 he had three of the five fastest miles ever run, but not a single one under four minutes. Then, of course, came the scandal linking him to numerous under-the-table payments and he was ruled ineligible for life. What a sad, sad way for a great runner's career to end.

That was the amateur ethos back then, right? It was very powerful.

It was. For example, when I became the first American to break four minutes I was invited to appear on a Saturday sport show out of New York called *Saturday Night Fights*. It was sponsored by Pabst Blue Ribbon Beer and they were going to fly me to New York and interview me live across the nation. But Avery Brundage, who was the president of the International Olympic Committee, told my coach that if I appeared on the same television show as professional boxers I was through, and that I would never race again.

Quite a different story from today, isn't it, where television and sponsorship basically control how track is presented and promoted.

It is. And it was frustrating at times to think about all the hard work we were doing but how at the end of the day it wasn't going to be worth a thing in terms of money or a job. It was a luxury, after all, just to get on a shoe list. That was when you knew you had arrived. I remember the first time I got a free pair of shoes from Adidas, boy did I think I was something special. But I knew going into track that my time spent running was going to be short. In saying that, though, Avery could have been a better leader. The facts of the matter were, the world was changing and sport was becoming more commercial. He should have recognized that instead of acting so stubborn. But Avery was going to defend that Olympic ideal to his grave, and he did. I have no regrets about my career and when it took place, though. It was an honor to run when I did. Those were such exciting times chasing the first four-minute mile. It was an absolute thrill.

So then you'd say it was maturing as a middle-distance runner in the age of Roger Bannister and the mystery of the four-minute mile that inspired you to become a miler?

Without a doubt. After Bannister's great race in 1954, I immediately began to think that breaking four minutes was something I'd like to give a go.

Yet you never ran the mile that year, your senior year of high school. Why not?

A couple of reasons. First, I was having a great deal of success with the half-mile. I was undefeated and I had set the national high school record. So I wasn't thinking about trying a new event or looking for success elsewhere. To be honest, I had about all that I could handle. But I also wouldn't have been physically capable of handling the mile in high school. I was quite tall [6-foot-3] and gangly [150 pounds], and not very strong. I was young for my age and needed time to mature. In fact, if I had been stronger in high school I wouldn't even have run track. I wanted to play football. But the football coach thought I'd get crushed to pieces the first time I got tackled. He said to me when I asked him about trying out, "Don, you're built like a rooster with no feathers. You'd get blown down by a good strong wind, let alone some nasty linebacker." And he was worried that I might get hurt because then my father, who was his dentist, might get revenge on him in the dentist's chair. So he encouraged me to begin running instead. And really, that was how I became a runner in the first place.

Why do you think it took so long following Bannister—more than three years, in fact—for an American to break four minutes for a mile?

That's a good question, and I can tell you that a lot of guys were wondering the same thing. Not only that, the press and the public were on us about it, too. And going back to that earlier question of yours, this was when four minutes did begin to become a nationalistic thing. Americans were doing a lot of great things in the world, and growing economically and so forth, but no American was under four minutes while a number of guys from different countries were. Everyone was asking, *Where are the Americans?* And once Santee got kicked out there was nobody to replace him at that four-minute level. Jerome Walters and Bob Seaman were probably our top guys but they couldn't seem to do it, and no one else was coming through the ranks. So that was an odd period in American distance running with no one at all among the world's top 10 milers.

Did this become something American milers were embarrassed by?

Oh, yeah. Guys were saying, *We gotta get someone to do this*. Especially when nations with far fewer people had done it, like England, Australia, Hungary, Ireland, Denmark.

Were you embarrassed by it?

To an extent I was. I mean, gee whiz, we were so good at every other event in track, and we were a big country with a lot of people, so we should have been able to put a man under four.

Did you consider it your personal duty to try to become the first American to run under four minutes?

Not at all. I was just a kid in the early '50s, remember. When Bannister first broke four, in 1954, I was only in high school. And the next year, 1955, I was just a freshman in college and I had only run the mile once in my whole life. So certainly the responsibility to get an American under four minutes couldn't have been mine. Then the year after that, 1956, my only goal was to make the Olympic team and compete in the games in Melbourne. So again, four minutes wasn't really something I was overly concerned with.

When did you begin thinking about making an assault on four minutes?

Well, to answer that I need to go back to 1956. As I'm sure you probably know, the Olympics that year were in Australia. And on account of the opposite seasons they were scheduled for December. That meant if I was to make the team I would have missed the fall semester of college. And my dad wasn't about to support that. No way was he going to allow athletics, not even the Olympic Games, interfere with my progress in school. He was pretty strict about matters like that. But I made a deal with him that I would attend summer school to get myself ahead, so if I made the Olympic team I wouldn't be behind when I returned to school the following spring. Anyway, he reluctantly agreed to that, which then put me on a brutal summer schedule of studying, training, and running qualifying races around the country. But to make a long story short, I did end up making the Olympic team when I outleaned Fred Dwyer in the final 1500 meter qualifying race. But because of my hectic summer routine I came down with mononucleosis in Melbourne and finished dead last in my heat. And I was really upset by that. So after the Olympics when I got back home, I began to think about a new goal to redeem myself, and breaking four minutes immediately came to mind. And because of all the hard work I had done in 1956 to make the Olympic team, I was in the best shape of my life entering the 1957 season. But becoming the first American to do it wasn't on my mind at all.

Why not?

I'm not sure. Maybe I was too modest, or unconfident, especially as I was still pretty much a newcomer to the mile. It really wasn't until that spring that I began to think I could be the first American miler to get under four. That was when Tom Courtney, who was the 1956 Olympic 800-meter champion, and a friend of mine from our time together over in Melbourne, came out from New York to do a few workouts with me at Cal. One session we did was a three-quarter-mile time trial in 2:57. And right after that Courtney was saying to everyone what great shape he was in and how he was going to be the first American to get under four. Which then made me think, *Hang on a minute, I just ran the same time trial with him, maybe I can become the first American under four.* And straightaway I asked Brutus what he thought, and he thought I had a good chance. So immediately we began preparing for it, and I increased my workload considerably. Because by this time a lot of guys were gearing up to try to break four. So there was definitely a sense of urgency in the air. We even picked the day I'd go for it: the first of June at a small meet in Stockton, the Pacific Association AAU Championships. And I knew I just had that one chance to get it done because Brutus had me scheduled to run half-miles the rest of the season.

Did you make your plans public?

No, it was strictly a private setup between Brutus and me. The way we looked at it, this was our own goal, no one else's. Even the meet promoter didn't know about our plans. In fact, my name wasn't on the initial start list for the mile. They had me down to run the half-mile. But when I started warming up for the mile the starter quickly added my name to the list.

Why didn't you decide to try to do it at one of the large California invitationals?

I wanted everything to be low-key: no rabbits, no crowds, no press. That's just the kind of guy I am. I'm not a big show guy. Brutus was the same. Also, I didn't want to have to fight through a lot of traffic, or worry about other guys in the race. It was too easy for me to get knocked around and thrown off balance. I was more comfortable leading and running up front. At Stockton, there wasn't going to be a lot of shoving and pushing. There were only four other runners in the race. Also, I had practiced my pacing really well and I thought a crowded race might disturb me, whereas in a smaller field I could control everything myself. I must say, I had that 60-second rhythm down pat. So much so that running at 60-second pace actually felt easier to me than running at say, 65-second pace.

How was that?

I know it sounds strange, but because of my long legs and big stride, I liked to be clear and free when I ran. If my stride was tight or bunched up everything felt harder, and I felt out of sync. So getting myself into that easy rhythm was crucial if I was going to run well. Then my body could just flow naturally. I used to run with a picture in my mind of this even distribution of energy, like a battery pulling a quiet, steady charge. I'd focus on that to remain relaxed and efficient. And that was exactly what I did in Stockton.

Now, I read recently that you almost didn't make it to Stockton that day. What happened?

Well, the morning of June 1 I had a three-hour economics final. And in studying for it I missed a few days of important training. So I began to wonder whether I should actually run. And all during the final I kept going back and forth in my mind, *Should I or shouldn't I run?* To make matters worse, outside the exam room, which was nearby the stadium, a high school track meet was taking place and every time the gun sounded I jumped in my seat think-ing about what I had planned for that afternoon. Anyway, when I finished the exam I decided to at least drive out to Stockton. Now, that was a hot, hot day in the valley, like so many days are. But always when the sun went down and the temperature dropped it felt like there was suddenly more oxygen in the air and it became easier to breathe. I realize that may not be correct sci-entifically, but that was how it felt to me. And that night in Stockton, I swear the air was loaded with oxygen. So when I stepped out of my car and took a deep breath, my decision was made: I was running.

. . . So the race started and you went straight to the lead?

I did, and immediately all my tiredness disappeared as I settled into my 60-second rhythm.

Was that your first lap split, 60?

Near enough. It was 59.7.

And you felt good?

Yeah, I knew I was in for a great race.

How did you know that?

Just from how easy and effortless I felt. Honestly, everything came togeth-er for me that night: The track was perfect, the air was clear and fresh, I found my rhythm. I was just very fortunate to have one of those days.

Did you hear your other splits as the race went on?

Oh, sure. Brutus was on the backstretch keeping me informed all the way. He was screaming, "You're right on, Don. Keep going." And I continued to hit the lap times I wanted, 2:00.8 at the half mile, and 3:00.6 at three-quar-ters. And all the while my confidence was growing because I wasn't feeling tired at all. That was the amazing thing about that race. Everything just came so easily. And besides Brutus yelling out my times, the track announcer, H. D. Thoreau, figured out pretty quickly that something special was happening, and he began urging me on, too. I could hear him building up the crowd, telling them that they were possibly witnessing the first American to break four minutes for a mile. And as he got more excited, I got more excited; he was actually screaming my splits over the loudspeaker. And when I entered the homestretch for the last time he began counting down. So here I was charging to the line with this voice all around me, "Three fifty-one, three fifty-two, three fifty-three . . . " and so on. And boy did that help; and I just kept pushing and pushing all the way to the tape.

And when you finished you knew you had done it?

I knew. I knew immediately that something special had just occurred. But right away I began worrying whether everything was going to be all right with the timing and so forth, and if the track had been measured properly. But as luck would have it, the meet promoter had measured the track that day just to make sure everything was fine.

Did you jump up and down or punch your fist in the air when you finally heard the official result?

Not so much anything like that. Someone handed me a big bouquet of flowers and I jogged around the track a couple of times. Naturally, I wanted to find Brutus and thank him, but being Brutus he had already left the stadium to help one of my teammates get ready for his race. That was Brutus for you, never taking any credit for what his athletes achieved, and always looking out for the next guy. Something interesting, though, was that right after my race the meet director presented me with the trophy for outstanding performance of the meet, even though the mile was the first event on the program. I thought that was a bit funny, but I accepted it all the same.

Did your life change in any way after that race?

I've always said that I felt blessed to be the first American sub-four-minute miler. That was a very special day, one of the highlights of my life. And not just because I made history as the first American to run under four minutes, but because I set a goal, worked for it, then made it happen. And whenever you can do that, whether it's in sport, or business, or anything else, it's always a fantastic moment. But you know, I had great support and stability in my family, so what I did that night in Stockton was quickly put into perspective. In other words, I remained pretty levelheaded about it all.

Did you expect a wave of American milers to follow you under four minutes? Because interestingly, another American didn't crack four minutes until two years later.

I did expect some guys to follow me under four minutes. But I guess it still remained a mental barrier for many of them. To believe in such a hard goal is tough. I know it took me a while to develop that internal confidence. Or maybe a lot of coaches didn't make the adjustments to help their athletes do it. Stampfl obviously had, and Brutus did. But things picked up by the early '60s, and eventually American milers were doing well again.

Yet your career was over by then, and amazingly you only ended up running that one four-minute mile. Why was that?

I had injury problems, especially my Achilles tendon, which I ruptured right before the 1960 Olympic trials. That's probably my greatest track disappointment, not being able to compete at my best in the Olympic Games. That's the trick with the Olympics: You have to be ready at the right time. There are no second chances. But I can't dwell on what could have been. I had a great career while it lasted. And there was almost no better time in my life than 1957: I was in great condition, and I was able to run free and push my body to its limit. That's an amazing feeling after all, to be working at your maximum and going on all cylinders like that. Really, it's something priceless.

Finally, Don, what do you think of today's runners' professional attitudes compared to your almost casual, part-time approach to athletics?

I believe we are all products of our times. Athletes today have to train full time in order to succeed. And they can't question that. It's natural for them. Just like one hour a day at the track was natural for me. I completely understand why guys today would never follow my or Brutus's philosophy. Although maybe the pendulum has shifted a bit too far to the other side. I still believe it's important to consider what running can teach you about yourself. Otherwise, won't sport just end up becoming just some frivolous obsession?

Photo: Sports Agence

# A Man in Charge

## HERB ELLIOTT
### (Australia)

**First sub-4: January 25, 1958, 3:59.9, Melbourne, Australia**
**Personal best: 3:54.5**
**Total sub-4s: 17**

*Images of Portsea, the rugged coastal landscape on the tip of Mornington Peninsula, 60 miles east of Melbourne, enter my mind—a bronzed body in white cotton shorts piling over sand dunes so driven and intense . . . feet bare slide beneath him, effectively doubling the effort required, the energy needed. Later he's lifting barbells fashioned out of slabs of cement; he's awake at dawn eating tasteless oatmeal; he's tumbling naked in the moonlit surf; and he's absorbing philosophy under a watchful eye: guided, mentored, nurtured to become a champion. Here was power and intelligence burning bright, the spark provided by his enigmatic coach, Percy Cerutty. The challenge they faced—quite simple, really—to prepare a man to run a mile. But not an ordinary mile, it must be said. This had to be a mile run with courage, where the athlete expends every bit of ambition, pride, and determination.*

*Australia's recent gold-medal success in sport is staggering: labs, gyms, coaches, and specialists from abroad—sport psychologists, biomechanists, physiologists. And yet there is still Portsea, where nature's varieties present challenge upon challenge. Is there really anything more that an athlete could demand?*

As a 16-year old boy, Herb, in early 1954, were you aware of the earnestness with which John Landy, your countryman, was trying to run the first-ever sub-four-minute mile?

Yes, I was. I took a great interest in the four-minute mile through the newspapers, and I was hoping like mad that Landy would beat Roger Bannister and Wes Santee to it. In fact, as a schoolboy I wrote to Landy asking for training advice.

Did he reply?

In seven or eight pages . . . with details on training and schedules to follow. It was brilliant. He even mentioned that he had heard of me—I was a junior runner at the time winning a few races. That really sparked me, I must say. John was always very generous, inspirational, and helpful to me.

Can you describe the mood in Australia as Landy approached four minutes?

It was fantastic. For all of John's races—and remember these were just simply organized twilight meetings—there would be 30,000 to 40,000 at Melbourne's Olympic Park. People would do anything to get a look. It was the anticipation that excited everyone. The desire to be there when he broke the four-minute mile. To see if it could be done; to see what might happen to him. It was like the way people tuned in the first space shoot. John and the four-minute mile completely captivated the imagination of the Australian public.

Why do you think that was? Why the public fascination with the four-minute mile?

It's an easy event to understand and to remember. People don't know what a good time is for other distances, but, *four minutes and a mile,* that hangs together somehow. You didn't need to be a sporting fanatic, either, to notice the developments that were occurring in the mile. Could a sub-four mile be run? Who would be first? Everyone was asking these questions. It was a special time for running. People were enchanted and engaged then by the pursuit of this clear barrier. For example, I don't even know what the world record for the mile is today.

You're serious?

Yes.

It's 3:43.13.

Wow! Who has that?

Honestly, you don't know?

No, which is my point. Just those numbers, three-four-three, they're hard to remember, not like four-zero-zero.

It's Hicham El Guerrouj, from Morocco.

Right.

So when did you start thinking that you could be a four-minute miler, and maybe as good as Landy?

Once I became serious about my running, in 1956, I was quite sure that I would eventually break four minutes. For me it was more a matter of when.

Still, was four minutes any sort of beacon for you?

I was concerned with progression. I wanted to continually run faster so, yes, in order to do that I needed targets, and without a doubt four minutes was a real target for me. It was a faster time than I had ever run before, but so was 4:04, or 4:02.

So nothing extra special about four minutes?

It was just another time to me. But of course, I couldn't ignore the hype around four minutes. I participated in it myself, didn't I, by writing to Landy and cheering for him to get there first?

Was your progression toward four minutes smooth, or did you have any hiccups along the way—the feeling of reaching a plateau or being stuck?

Actually, I had the toughest time getting past 4:06. I first ran 4:06 in January 1957. It was a world junior record and 14 seconds better than my previous best. I was chuffed. That was also when Landy first acknowledged me publicly with a review of my performance in the *Melbourne Argus*. But this new junior record got me hung up on times and barriers for a wee while. Two weeks later I ran 4:06 again, this time beating the great Ron Clarke. Then the next week in the South Australian Mile Championship in Adelaide, I ran another 4:06. And again a few weeks later in Sydney, 4:06.

Were you getting impatient?

It was definitely bothersome. In fact, I was so determined to get past that bloody 4:06 that I set up a time trial where I tried to run four laps in 60 seconds each to test my ability to run four minutes. Well, that went all wrong, and I walked off the track when I heard 3:06 after three laps. But once I began to remind myself about my philosophy toward running, which was basically, *Run hard; don't worry about records,* I began to relax and feel calmer. And the next week I ran 4:04 and felt like I was back on track with my progressions.

And then at the end of that season, in March 1957, at the Australian Championships, you ran 4:00.4.

I beat Merv Lincoln in a very exciting race. I took the lead with a lap remaining and literally ran scared all the way to the line.

Your season ended there, though. Didn't you consider carrying on to try to break four minutes?

No. I was ready for a break. I knew that eventually I'd get under four. So I got stuck into my training instead. Over that winter and spring of 1957 I ran hundreds and hundreds of miles out at Portsea and lifted thousands of pounds of weights.

This is the period in your career that you refer to in your book *The Golden Mile* with the chapter heading, "A Body Built on Pain." Sounds a bit harsh, Herb.

Not when all that stands in the way of running fast is your tolerance to pain. I saw pain as cleansing and compassionate.

Compassionate?

And purifying. When you can walk away from a tough training session knowing that you've come out the other end all right, you leave with a clear conscience. You leave knowing that you can look death in the eye.

Interestingly, in another chapter in your book you suggest the need for an entirely different attitude with the title "A Lazy Bloke in Cardiff." Could you comment on the oscillation from extreme sacrifice and stoicism, to living it up and having a good time?

I needed releases, and I was never afraid to have a break. I certainly don't believe that a week or two of high living can ruin a season.

What made Portsea special, the coastal training camp operated by your coach Percy Cerutty?

It was demanding, incredibly so. But also inspirational, natural, and beautiful. We had elaborate circuits and routes through the sand dunes . . . Percy had designed them to test our spirit and commitment to running.

Going back to 1957, Herb, with a hard winter's training at Portsea behind you, you came to Melbourne on January 25, 1958, your first mile of the season, and you broke four minutes for the first time [3:59.9].

That race went pretty easily. I trailed the pack for two laps and when I heard the half-mile time [2:01] I decided to run the rest of the race by myself. And I can say that I was pleased at the finish.

That's a bit of an understatement isn't it? Suddenly you're a four-minute-miler.

But explicit timed targets were never my real aim. I was very harsh on myself in terms of wanting to improve, but in the front of my mind I never allowed myself to impose any limits on what I could achieve.

So the fact that you began the 1958 season not even a sub-four-minute miler and then went on to become the mile world record holder by the end of the year didn't surprise you?

Entering the 1958 season I had the feeling that within me there was enormous power and capability, and that I was going to improve my mile time from the previous year. Also, I was prepared to work as hard as I possibly could.

Was it Cerutty who influenced you to ignore times and not impose limits on yourself?

He always warned me about making too big a deal out of a time because he felt the satisfaction you'd get once you achieved that time might be so great that you might not want to go on.

And that would be bad?

Of course, because then you would have never truly tested yourself, your ability, your strength; and to Percy—and I agree with this—that would be a waste. It's amazing to me that a person could sustain himself just by wanting to run a fast time. To devote a lot of your life to something as trivial as that without having some bigger context seems narrow to me. That was why I always tried to see running as a means for me to grow and develop as a person. That always gave me more of reason for doing it, especially when it started to get tough and I began asking myself, *Why am I putting up with all of this pain and discomfort?* But the thing is, I always had an answer to that question: *To become a better person.*

If times weren't so important to you as a miler, was competition and beating others?

My countryman and rival Merv Lincoln was a huge influence in this regard. Without Merv around to provide competition, I may not have been so driven. There was this edge between us that kept me sharp and focused in my training. And there were quite a number of times when I had Merv in my mind when I was out training.

What else was in your mind when you ran?

Only one thing, *Keep going.* In training, I always felt the temptation to slow down. I'd think to myself, *You're going too fast. You're not going to finish.* That's when Merv would appear in my mind, or else some faceless competitor. For example, I might be running up a hill with 2 miles to go in a 10-mile training session and I'd be in so much discomfort that I'd think I was never going to reach the top. Now you can imagine the temptation to slow down at this point; it was enormous. But then I'd see this faceless competitor on my shoulder who could see into my heart and into my mind and could sense the weakness and was ready to pounce. That image kept me going through a lot of hard workouts.

Was that the case in races, too? You concocted a phantom competitor to guard against your vulnerabilities?

By the time I got to a race I had spent a lot time visualizing someone on my shoulder just ready to pass me, and because I hadn't let him pass me a million times in training it became instinctive in races.

Sounds like you're an advocate of sport psychology?

I am, but not under that name. I think there is a danger when you introduce more science into sport, although I admit that you have to. But it does make it harder to keep the spiritual part of yourself alive when guys in lab coats are drawing your blood or computer digitalizing your gait.

Can athletes be artists, Herb?

Why not? Running is everything that we are. Our mental, spiritual, and physical sides all united. But when I try to tell that to young Australians today they look at me as if I'm some silly old new-age fool. My stories of how I approached running don't seem to resonate or touch them in any way. I can sense that from their faces, and it amazes me. No one lights up at all when I describe Portsea or Percy. Not a single one of them. No one exhibits any sympathy or empathy for the subjects I raise, or my philosophy for running. I don't think they see any truth in it. It has no meaning or significance in today's world, or in their lives or ambitions. What matters to them, it seems, are split times, records, and standards.

And money?

That too. Whereas I ran practically for free.

Do any circumstances today, Herb, trigger inside you some recollection of being a young miler again and feeling what you just described: whole and complete mentally, spiritually, and physically?

I can't run anymore because of too many aches and pains, so it's not that. But I might be driving along a country road somewhere and all of sudden there's this clean cut through the forest where they've put in cable poles or something that goes up a steep hill and off into the distance. And when I see that I get a "hot" feeling in my lungs, like I used to experience when I was running hard. Those were the times in my life when I was at my limit, but also on top of it all.

So the years of training and racing are still part of you?

I do get nostalgic about the past and my life and times as a miler. But it's not something I wallow in. All those experiences I had running can't be forgotten just like that. In many ways, they're who I am.

Obviously another important moment besides your first sub-four, Herb, was when you set the mile world record on August 6, 1958, in Dublin [3:54.5]. How did that race eventuate?

It wasn't planned, that I can tell you. The big event for me that summer was the Empire Games in Cardiff. After that I wasn't too fussed about the rest of my season. So I don't have any recollection of that race being part of my program where I would attempt a fast time. But maybe Percy or some of the Australian team officials negotiated it. But anyway, all of a sudden it was in front of me and I had just spent a week boozing and letting my hair down after the Empire Games. Initially, preparing to run some ordinary race straight after winning two gold medals at the Empire Games felt very anti-climatic and more like an obligation. But in the bus on the way to the stadium I couldn't believe how many people were about and I thought, *My God, this is serious.* Of course, the Irish wanted to see their hero Ronnie Delany thrash me. But my fitness and extreme buildup for the Empire Games was luckily still inside me waiting to be let loose.

So what did you do to get focused?

Well, we came up with a plan to try to beat Delany. Alby Thomas, my teammate, would lead for two laps and then Merv Lincoln would take over and he and I would fight it out to the end. That's pretty much how it went, with a very fast last lap [54 seconds].

Did the world record change you, or make you feel part of some special tradition?

I never felt any sense of ownership when I held the mile world record, if that's what you mean, or that I suddenly belonged to an exclusive club. It was just another time, another progression. But obviously there was a sense of, *My God, nobody has ever run faster than I just have.* But I don't remember being knocked about by it too much.

What about other people—did you find that your achievements effected the way people treated you?

To be quite honest, I could never quite understand why people would meet me and get so gushy. I was really surprised by that, and couldn't understand it at all because I knew that I was a pretty ordinary bloke, as are most all of the other champions in sport I've met.

Do you believe that you were particularly suited—physiologically, psychologically speaking—to the mile, or did you suit yourself to it because it was the mile?

I was particularly suited to the mile, and only the mile. Because if I could have won medals and set records over 100 meters I would have done that because it's easier. I've always said that a marathon runner is someone who has tried everything else and failed. You get your success in the easiest possible way.

So then, do you think your "style" as a miler—the way you trained and raced—was somehow an expression of your personality? That is, the type of person you were?

I would describe myself as intense and persistent. When I'm faced with a choice I like to consider my options, make a quick decision, and then just really belt it.

Herb, I can't help but be amazed by your 1958 season so I want to return to that. How did that year feel to you because ostensibly you had three seasons. The summer season in Australia [January-March], the spring season in the United States [May-June], and the summer season in Europe [July-August]. And in that short time you became the greatest miler in the world.

It was a busy time, and long, but it wasn't a burden for me. And it didn't feel frenzied or hectic. Again, I was just training and preparing myself to run faster and that's what I did.

I think I already know the answer to this question but I'll ask you anyway. Did you have any superstitions or odd pre-race habits?

Definitely not.

That's what I thought. But what gave you the confidence that you were ready to run fast? Did you have a particular workout that indicated you were fit and in form?

At Portsea we had tests to measure our fitness, but from Percy's point of view it was ridiculous to be constantly testing yourself against the clock. That showed a lack of confidence in the intelligent decisions you had made with regard to your training, and with the intensity and dedication that you'd applied to your training. If you constantly wanted to test yourself against the clock, that showed a total lack of confidence. So we would go for weeks without timing ourselves, just doing our training and doing it hard and going for it. I feel sorry for people who have this incredible fascination with the clock. Every day to have to answer to the clock must make training so boring.

The tyranny of time.

Plus the clock's terribly misleading. If actually what you're trying to do to be a good miler is develop mental toughness and strength—which is basically what you should be trying to do because anybody with any aptitude as a miler can run a quarter mile in 51 or 52 seconds—the key to success is somehow to keep running at that pace over four laps, and to do that you have to develop toughness, not watch a clock. Or as another example, imagine it's just one of those days and you wake up to go for your run and your chemistry's not right and you feel tired and you're dragging your arse along the ground and you're training mercilessly to try to keep going but it's just bloody sheer hard work. A bloody hard grind. Well, if you had a clock on yourself you might see that your time's a bit slow and then think, *That session was a waste.* When in fact, it was the best you'd ever done given the circumstances and the toughness you displayed in working through a bad day.

So for you feedback was an internal experience?

Yes. That's right.

Could Percy read your reactions and determine how you were progressing?

He was never terribly interested in what I was doing in my training. He was more interested in my state of mind. If I was enthusiastic, dedicated, and intelligent then he'd just pop in every now and then, like once a week, to have a look at what I was up to. He didn't care too much about the details of my training as long as I had my mind right.

But when a timed test was called for, what would you do?

There was this hilly circuit at Portsea called the Hall Circuit. It was a mile and one-quarter or something like that carved out of sand and scrub and ti-trees. I'd just belt myself around that and see how the time was and if the time was an improvement on the last time then I'd think, *Oh, yeah, everything's going okay.*

And if it was slower?

Then I'd ask myself why and begin considering the details of my program and what might need changing. But it wasn't this scientific scrutiny, it was more philosophical.

Percy was truly a scholar, wasn't he?

You only had to look at the guy's library to see how many interests he had. Science, art, history . . . and everything he read he applied to success on the track. When he talked about any of those things you'd be totally inspired. At least I was, and without him I never would have run as fast as I did.

The future of the mile, Herb?

Guys will just keep getting faster, I suppose.

Photo by Ed Lacey

# Driven Ahead

## PETER SNELL
### (New Zealand)

First sub-4: January 27, 1962, 3:54.4, Wangunui, New Zealand
Personal best: 3:54.03
Total sub-4s: 15

*P*eter Snell lives in America today. In the mid-1960s, as his athletic career was winding down, he began a course of study that eventually saw him earn a Ph.D. in exercise physiology and a permanent position on the faculty of the Southwest Dallas Medical School. He is Doctor Peter Snell now, and it's studying the genetic basis of physical activity that stirs his passions. What are the responses to exercise in aging populations? Can messenger RNA induced by physiological stress be measured? Science serves well the inquisitive mind: Discoveries incite further questions, and new questions beget bolder experiments, and on and on progress marches. Scientific theories, therefore, are just passing moments in time. Peter Snell's mantle in the history of the mile, though, is fixed and secure.

As a young New Zealander in leather spike shoes, cinders rose to the sky behind his speed and power. Tracks were gashed, torn, and ripped by his force; his competitors ground to dust. And so he traveled the world amid a whirlwind of victories and records.

*He was a triumph who always returned home glorious and successful.*

*Today Dr. Snell visits New Zealand regularly. The 16-hour flight brings him into season's opposite. At home he runs through the Auckland Domain where he trained as a rising Olympian and future world record holder. He visits Arthur Lydiard, his aging coach who revolutionized middle-distance running with his marathon training system. They might discuss past races, or today's champions' results. He tastes the foods of his youth, and smells the smells—ocean breezes, sheep paddocks; he embraces friends and family who surround him. Their gentle Kiwi twang warms his ears and stirs his memory. And in rolling green pasture and thick native bush he can shake free the foreign elements and attitudes of Dallas. He can track the past and escape his "otherness." New Zealand is where he can absorb comfort, familiarity, and home.*

Peter, do you think your "style" as a miler—the way you trained and raced—was in some way an expression of your personality?

As a boy I was certainly introverted, not flamboyant, and so I suppose well suited to solitary activities like running and so on. But I also had a tremendous need to excel and achieve. That more than anything, I think, was the vital drive I possessed, and what literally fueled my ambitions as a runner. I received much encouragement and attention through sport . . . and I immediately channeled all of my energy in that direction. In terms of racing style, I wanted to be a kicker. I grew up watching the rivalry between Roger Bannister and John Landy, and Bannister always won because he had the strongest finish. Naturally, I thought that a powerful homestretch drive was very important. In fact, as a kid I got beaten twice in the final straight so my thinking quickly turned to speed, speed, speed. I just loved to sit and kick. Really, I think every runner does.

But Arthur Lydiard, your coach, was famous for pushing middle-distance runners to engage in endurance training not speed training.

He was, thank God. It wasn't until I came under Arthur that I really began to develop. In 1957, when I was 18 and training on my own, my best half-mile time was only 2:00. Three years later with Arthur I was the Olympic champion with a best time of 1:46.

What changes did Arthur make to your training?

I became much more serious over the winter months in terms of going for long runs. For example, 22 miles on a Sunday over the Auckland ranges became a regular part of my week. And I raced more cross-country, too. Arthur always set me the target of running 100 miles in a week. Although I have to say that I rarely achieved that.

Do you believe that you were particularly suited—physiologically or psychologically speaking—to the mile, or did you suit yourself to it because it was the mile?

Actually, over my whole career, in terms of times and victories, I think I was best performed over the half mile. But after I set my first mile world record in Wangunui in 1962 I was never invited to run the half mile again. Everyone wanted to see me run the mile. Which is understandable given the mile's stature. And that was fine with me, too. But to say I had a genetic predisposition or otherwise to be a miler, I'm not so sure. Like I said, my desire to succeed was huge; I craved attention and recognition; probably that was the most important factor behind my gold medals and world records.

Do you know that you are only one of three runners whose first sub-four-minute mile was also a new world record?

I didn't know that actually, but I suppose that's true. Bannister and Landy would be the other two?

That's right. So approaching the race in Wangunui, your first sub-four, were you thinking about setting a new world record or just getting below four minutes?

Since high school I had wanted to be a four-minute miler. I regarded it as a crucial landmark in any middle-distance runner's progress. So in my mind it was important to get it done. The early emphasis I placed on the half mile was due to my poor background in endurance training, not a disregard for the mile. But in 1958, after my first winter of distance running under Arthur,

I ran a mile in 4:10.2, which represented a big improvement on my previous best time. And the next winter [1959] my performances were much better at cross-country [4th in the New Zealand championships versus 55th in 1958]. So I felt that that summer I might possibly break four minutes. However, a stress fracture in my tibia interrupted my training for eight weeks, and Arthur and I decided that due to my limited endurance base, I should concentrate on the half mile for the 1960 Olympic season. It wasn't until after the Olympics that I had another opportunity to run a mile and I ran a personal best, 4:01.5, in Dublin. But due to my 800-meter gold medal, I was typecast as a half-miler, and I just couldn't get into any more mile races . . .

And you actively wanted to break out of that half-mile mold?

I did. And heading into the New Zealand winter of 1961 I really concentrated on distance training for four solid months. And the results were amazing. In my first week of track training a week after running a marathon on December 9, I ran a fast three-quarter-mile time trial. I knew then I was capable of a fast mile. This was confirmed on January 1 when I ran 4:02 in a small town on the South Island of New Zealand called Timaru. Now I was sure that with a few more weeks of track training and some races at 880 yards, I would be capable of running well under four minutes, perhaps even as fast as 3:57. At that point it was just a question of picking the venue. I definitely wanted to do it in New Zealand, though, because a sub-four-minute mile had never been run in New Zealand at this point. This was my opportunity to present the New Zealand public with a gift: their first four-minute mile. Wangunui, then, was purely about running my first four-minute mile as well as the first four-minute mile in New Zealand. I never had any concerns or doubts about winning the race or breaking four minutes. It was only a question of by how much.

That must have been a nice position to be in?

Yes, it was. But to be honest, the 3:54 shocked me. Like I said, I imagined running 3:57, but not really any faster than that.

*How did it feel, then, to suddenly become the mile world record holder?*

It was a great honor, and really a very big deal to me. Actually, it's unfortunate that I wasn't more conscious of working hard and pushing the pace in that race because I think I could have run even faster. I had way too much energy left at the finish. But in no way did I feel that I had squandered some once-in-a-lifetime opportunity. I believed without a doubt that I'd have further opportunities down the line to run faster. I think I was only around 3:00 at the three-quarters, so my last lap was very fast.

*What sensations did you have running that very fast last lap?*

I remember going down the backstretch for the final time and really just giving up control of myself. I simply let go and absolutely poured it on. Up to that point in my running, I don't think that I had ever felt such a glorious feeling of strength and speed without strain.

*How was the atmosphere in Wangunui that night?*

Marvelous. That was an old grass track, you know. It was also 385 yards, not a normal quarter-mile track. And it was a late start, I think 9:30, so we ran under bright floodlights. But the grounds were jammed. In fact, that race has become one of those epic events that hundreds of thousands of people say they saw, when it fact it was closer to 20,000. But there was even a bigger crowd a few weeks later in Auckland when I ran my second four-minute mile [3:56.8].

*Was that your gift to the people of Auckland?*

That's right. Yes, it was. And they came out in droves. Which was very nice. In fact, there's a story about the crowd at that race, too. Apparently, people were so excited that they were rushing in and paying their money at the gate without even waiting to collect their change.

*So, Peter, when you look back like this on your career, especially your world records and gold medals, what strikes you the most about everything you achieved?*

Actually, when I consider my career today I find it frightening.

How so?

It's just incredible, almost sickening really, how focused, self-centered, and one-dimensional I was. And that couldn't have been a good thing. Anything that didn't have to do with running I disregarded from my life. I did terribly in school, my social life was limited, I had no hobbies or interests. Every decision I made or others made for me was intended to see what I could achieve as a runner.

Perhaps that's what it takes to be a champion?

In some respects I believe it does, and that's the scary part. To handle Arthur's training I had to adopt what I would almost call survival tactics or instincts—it was that demanding, not to mention boring and repetitious. I find it hard when young athletes ask me what they need to do to win an Olympic medal or set a world record. Do I want to influence someone down that path? Because honestly, I'm not convinced it's that healthy to sacrifice becoming an interesting or well-rounded individual in the hopes of becoming a sport star. That's an awfully big gamble to take. Of course it's great if you pull it off. But what if you don't? And I don't believe any of that bullshit about the struggle being worth the sacrifice even if you don't get the results. To my mind, that's just crazy thinking.

Are you saying you regret the choices you made as a young man?

Heavens no. And I'm grateful that I didn't have to listen to what people say today about the importance of living a balanced life. Because if I had tried to do that, I never would have been so successful. What I accomplished required a complete and total commitment. It was the only way I was going to be able to pull it off. Today, though, I'm very careful about what I do and don't do. I won't live again like I did as a runner . . . I don't want my work to become such an obsession, and I don't want to be so one-dimensional. I have too many outside interests now. And I want to continue to enjoy them. In many ways, I think that's a better way to lead one's life. But will it produce a champion runner or the world's most famous exercise physiologist? Probably not.

Was your life as a runner really that restrictive? Because in reading your book *No Bugles, No Drums,* it seems as if you were part of a continuous whirlwind of racing and traveling. Surely that must have been exciting and glamorous as a young New Zealand man?

That's literature, isn't it? I agree with you, though, the book does give that impression. But my career wasn't like that at all. Basically, it was just one successive period of hard boring work followed by another. In saying that, though, New Zealand society back then was fairly dull. There were few career choices, there was no television, travel was limited. I didn't see myself having many other options for filling my day besides running. Today, of course, that's all changed. And it makes perfectly good sense to me why we have such a decline in great Western milers. Life is too prosperous to tolerate all that hard work.

You said as a boy that there weren't many exciting options for young people in New Zealand, but did you have any early running heroes who excited you about the sport?

Bannister, of course, was someone whose career I followed. Also, in New Zealand we had these biographies and stories of great runners by British writers . . . and I read them all. One that really stands out in my mind is the Emil Zatopeck story. He fascinated me. As did the great Hungarian milers who were so dominant in the late 1950s. We did get *Track and Field News* in New Zealand, so I kept up with the sport that way, too. But what excited me more than anything was seeing my own name in the newspaper. That was always such a thrill and, with my high-achiever personality, something that really kept me motivated and driven to succeed.

Is there anything in particular about being a young, ambitious miler that you miss today?

Yes: the exhilaration of speed. That's something I miss a great deal. For example, when I'm back in New Zealand I always revisit my old running loops and make my way around them for old time's sake. And what utterly amazes me is how little everything has changed. It all looks exactly as it did 40 years ago . . . the layout, the growth. The only difference is me. And unfortunately I'm not a young miler in peak condition anymore. I'm an old miler with sore knees. But every now and then in the middle of a run, I might string together a couple of strides that feel absolutely perfect . . . like I'm back in my prime. And that feeling, to be honest, is what keeps me running today. I want to be able to enjoy the experience of striding out as long as possible.

Speaking of striding out, how much lower do you think the mile world record can go?

Not much. And there are compelling physiological principles to support this. Success as a distance runner is mainly an energy production problem, or what's referred to as oxygen transport. Initially, it was believed that performance in endurance events was limited by cardiovascular capacity and how much blood, and therefore oxygen, could be pumped through the body to all the working muscles. But now the key limitation seems to be the amount of oxygen that can be transferred from the lungs to the blood. In other words, athletes' cardiovascular capacity is so high today that their blood rushes through their lungs before becoming completely saturated with oxygen. More than anything else, that's a lung membrane problem. And I don't see how much change can occur at that membrane level. And of course, without the ability to deliver more oxygen to working muscles, a runner will only have so much energy to continue improving. But I must say, these great African milers like [Hicham] El Guerrouj have perfect bodies. They look like racehorses or greyhounds . . . their lean torso, strong legs, and voluminous oxygen capacity. They're amazing. And it's fantastic that the Africans even want to run the mile, an event they didn't grew up with. That fact alone reflects the prestige of the mile and its celebrity. And let me just say, I'm very pleased that such a great race has retained its significance and importance as a world event.

# A Devoted Miler

## JOHN DAVIES
### (New Zealand)

**First Sub-4: February 15, 1963, 3:58.8, Dunedin, New Zealand**
**Personal best: 3:56.80**
**Total Sub-4s: 8**

*T he Pacific Ocean is flat today, and the beaches running beside the road are vacant: school's in session, work's downtown. I'm driving through a small suburb outside Auckland. I'm here to see John Davies.*

*I've met John before, and I've already made up my mind about him. I like him. He speaks in wise self-reflexive tones about sport and people. He's interested in the bigger issues facing sport, too, like doping and professionalism. When I knock on his door he's finishing his lunch. He extends his right hand and directs me inside; in his left hand a plate tilts and crumbs drop to the floor. I take my coffee black and we sit down on a soft couch. Traffic outside passes; his wife moves through their small garden pulling weeds and sweeping the ground. John begins to speak easily about his past. Winter is approaching in New Zealand, and the light is slightly dim.*

*I had to visit this land whose middle-distance runners once ruled the world. For two Olympics—1960, 1964—New Zealand's sporting tradition was track: Snell (three golds), Halberg (one gold), Magee (one bronze). And all of them were Arthur Lydiard's boys, the hardscrabble coach who invented marathon training and turned a collection of neighborhood kids into world beaters. John Davies was there, too, winning a bronze medal of his own in 1964. And it's that era and what it meant to him that I'm keen to understand.*

John, Landy versus Bannister in 1954 to decide who would become the first man to break four minutes for the mile, were you supporting your "Down Under" compatriot, Landy?

Well, you know, Jim, I was born in England and came out to New Zealand as a young boy. So in effect, I had connections to both John and Roger.

So who were you behind?

I don't think I viewed the race to four minutes as a direct competition between Bannister and Landy, or between the Northern Hemisphere and the Southern Hemisphere. I saw it as a grand human obstacle or barrier. A bit like reaching the summit of Mount Everest, which Edmund Hillary had only done two years prior. That was how most people saw the pursuit of four minutes: an achievement to benefit all of mankind.

Do you remember how you heard that Bannister had done it?

I was in my first year of boarding school in 1954. And in the school's recreation room there was a large wooden dais where the headmaster laid out the newspaper every morning. And on the morning of May 7, there was the headline, ROGER BANNISTER RUNS FIRST FOUR-MINUTE MILE. And I'll tell you, I was staggered. Not just because it was a huge thing for someone to break four minutes, but in reading the report it came across to me that Bannister had really put himself through a tremendous physical barrier to achieve this feat. My recollection of the words in the story were that he went color blind and couldn't speak for 10 minutes. Well that just had me enthralled. And I remember thinking, *My God, is that what running a sub-four-minute mile does to you?* I was just amazed that someone could actually go through such a physical ordeal and come out the other end all right. Of course, the picture that accompanied the story added to the mystique. I'm sure you've seen it: Bannister's just crossed the line with his head off to one side and he's about to collapse except for a group of men supporting him. It's not hard to imagine the impression it would have made. Because there it was right in front of me, demonstrable evidence that Bannister had suffered terribly in bringing about this feat.

Were you already a runner by this time, or was it Bannister who inspired you to take up track?

I began running when I was living in England, and I carried on with it when we came out to New Zealand. At my high school there was a competition called the Distance Cup. It was held over the course of the school year and consisted of four races—a quarter-mile, half-mile, mile, and cross-country. Whom ever earned the most points across all those races won the Distance Cup. It was very prestigious, and bitterly contested. It took me several years to win it, in fact. So while I was already a runner in 1954, it was reading about Bannister's big day that inspired me to become a miler.

So he was your boyhood running hero?

No, my boyhood running hero was Herb Elliott, actually, the great Australian miler. I thought his Olympic 1500-meter victory in Rome in 1960 was one of the most impressive races ever run. The way he took control halfway and opened up a huge gap, and then broke the world and Olympic records . . . amazing. A feature-length movie comprised of highlights of those games was released a few months later. And as soon as I could I went to see it. I arrived for the first showing at two o'clock, and afterward I was so excited and inspired that I decided to watch it again. So I bought another ticket for the five o'clock show, and when that show ended I bought another ticket for the eight o'clock show. So I watched the same movie three times in one day just to see my hero Herb Elliott.

But your countrymen Peter Snell and Murray Halberg won gold medals in Rome, too. Why weren't they your heroes?

My relationship to Pete and Murray was different from that to Herb. I saw Pete as a contemporary of mine, and I suppose in some ways a rival. And Murray was more my mentor. He was someone I listened to, followed, and respected. He would talk to me about what I needed to do to keep improving, and how I should start training the Lydiard way. He was always gracious and generous with his time. For instance, in 1961 I raced Murray in a limited-handicap mile where the best runner in the race, Murray in this case, ran a full mile and everyone else had a handicap. My best mile at this stage was 4:20, and Murray, of course, had broken four minutes. So I was given a 40-yard handicap over Murray. On the last lap, though, I was still in the lead and running in front of Murray. And I was thinking, *Wow, this is great.* But when I hit the final homestretch I could hear the crowd building and I knew it could only mean one thing: Murray was chasing me down. And sure enough with about 50 yards to go he flashed past me, but he gave me such a startle that I had this huge rush of adrenaline and sprinted past him and won the race. Now, to be honest, the whole event was a bit of a setup for Murray, but he wasn't bothered at all. Which he could have been because first prize was a beautiful silver tea service that was really meant for him. In fact, it was following that race that Murray introduced me to Arthur Lydiard. And I was so excited after meeting Arthur and listening to him talk about running, that when I got back home I decided I was going to begin running one-hundred miles a week. And it took me about four months to get there but I eventually did.

What kind of training had you been doing previous to that?

Nothing very much, really. I'd go down to the track and run a few intervals, or maybe a mile or two continuous. There wasn't much information back then on training theory or sport science. The only book I came across was Franz Stampfl's guide to interval training, where he said you should start off the season by running 10 times 440 yards at 70 seconds and every week drop your time by a second until you can run all 10 under 60 seconds. Then you'd supposedly be ready to run a sub-four-minute mile. Well, that didn't work too well for me. In fact, early on in my career I found the mile to be a real struggle. Over the third lap I just suffered. But after a year of training the Lydiard way I had a breakthrough, and in one race in 1962 I improved

JOHN DAVIES 79

my mile time from 4:15 to 4:02.

The spirit and camaraderie associated with Lydiard and his training techniques must have been fantastic?

It was amazing what a difference his marathon training system made. In that 4:02 race, for example, my splits were all my fastest ever in a mile. When I heard my half-mile time, for example, which was 2:01, my first thought was, *Wow, incredible.* Because I could still remember, you see, when 2:01 was my best time for a half-mile, and here I was running that fast en route to a mile. But Lydiard's training enabled me to feel comfortable and in control, especially over the third lap.

What kind of personal relationship did you have with Arthur?

Because I didn't live in Auckland he largely coached me by mail. So we didn't communicate all that regularly on a one-to-one basis. But I would drive up to Auckland occasionally on Sundays to run with the other guys over Arthur's famous 22-mile loop in the Waitakeri Ranges. And afterward we'd all go back to Arthur's house for a cup of tea and a chat. Those were great times, really. And even though all of us were great rivals on the track, we were also good mates.

Now, you said 1962 was a breakthrough season for you, largely because your mile time dropped 13 seconds to 4:02. Was it also that year that breaking four minutes became a real goal for you?

I was convinced that I'd knock off four minutes in 1962. Arthur was sure I'd do it, too, and he was touting me as New Zealand's next sub-four-minute miler after Murray and Pete. He even included me on a five-race tour of America that he had organized, thinking that I'd get it done there. But things didn't quite go my way on that tour.

Did you have any close calls?

I did, actually, on the final race of the tour, in Los Angeles at the Mount

SAC Relays; I missed breaking four minutes by a whisper. In that race were all the best American milers—Jim Beatty, Jim Grelle, Cary Weisiger, Bill Dotson. And boy, did they go for it that afternoon. I was running my hardest just to keep in contact. But they were too tough, and I ended up finishing back in fifth place. But I wasn't disappointed because I knew the time was fast, and I thought maybe, just maybe I had squeaked under four. Afterward, then, waiting around for the results I was very nervous. Then finally the track announcer came on the PA and read off the results of the mile. "And in fifth place," he said, "from New Zealand, John Davies, with a time of three minutes and 59.8 seconds." Well, immediately Murray and I began dancing around and I just thought this was the greatest day of my life. But then about half an hour later, the announcer came back on the PA to say that the results of the mile had been revised. "And in fifth place," he began again, "from New Zealand, John Davies, with a time of four minutes and zero-point-two seconds." And, oh my goodness, I was terribly, terribly disappointed.

At the same time you must have thought, *Well, I'm right there. I'll definitely do it sooner or later.*

It wasn't that so much as breaking four minutes became an even more important goal in my mind; it became my total focus and reason for racing. But following a couple of other near misses, I decided that running solely to hit a time was too dull and uninspiring. And it was then that I realized what kind of runner I was. I realized I was someone who needed competition. I loved racing well against people, not the clock. Whether I won or lost didn't matter so much, it was just the idea of trying to beat someone that got me excited. So the fact that I had the opportunity to race Pete as much as I did, the greatest miler of my generation, the Olympic champion and world-record holder, was absolutely fantastic. And boy did I love having a go at beating him.

Wasn't it racing against Peter that you finally ran your first four-minute mile?

It was, in February 1963, at a meet in Dunedin, which is a city at the bottom of the South Island. And where I went to boarding school, too. So in effect racing there was like running in my hometown. And did you know that Queen Elizabeth was there, too?

You're kidding, at the track meet?

Yes, she was touring New Zealand at the time and because Peter Snell was our most famous athlete, she was obliged, I suspect, to go watch him run. Which was great for us because she created added interest in the meeting and we had a sold-out crowd.

Did you get to meet her?

I didn't, and I'll tell you why. The track we were going to run on in Dunedin was brand new, and something very different for New Zealand. The surface was hard, almost like asphalt, whereas every other track in New Zealand was soft. And when I went to inspect the track a few hours before my race, I realized that my spikes were too long and wouldn't sink far enough down. Now, these spikes were built into the soles of my shoes, and no way could I run in them. But at this late stage I didn't know what to do. At the same time, I was supposed to be attending a pre-meet garden party to meet the queen. In the end, though, I just had to give the queen a miss, and I went out and bought a file and sat in my hotel room for two hours filing my spikes down to the right size. So that's why I didn't get to meet the queen.

At least you had plenty of time to create a race plan.

Well, that's right.

So what was the plan? Was this going to be a deliberate attempt at four minutes?

Yes and no. Someone was lined up to pace the first lap, and Pete and I talked a little bit about what to do after that. We agreed that I'd take the second lap and he'd take the third. So, yes, I was keen to do the time. But I was more concerned with racing Pete and trying to beat him. Anyway, when the gun went off the pacemaker did his job and ran 58 seconds for the first lap. Then I took over. And I was barreling along and feeling quite comfortable as we passed the half mile in 1:59. Straightaway Pete took over and I was thinking to myself, *Oh, this is real good, we're really moving . . . and everyone's doing his job*. But down the backstretch of the third lap I started to realize that Pete wasn't going hard enough. So I screamed at him, "Come on, Pete, pick it up." At the same time, I noticed that he was looking tired and heavy. And by this point, with roughly a lap and a half remaining, I was getting concerned about four minutes and staying on schedule. So I decided to pass Pete to keep things moving. Also, in the back of my mind I knew that the only way to beat Pete was to surprise him and try to open up a quick gap. Because if there was one thing I knew about racing Peter Snell, it was that once he made his move and took the lead there was no passing him. If you waited for him to strike, you were dead. So there I was in the lead as we went through the bell. And I was still in the lead as we headed down the backstretch for the last time. And I'll tell you, Jim, I was going for it. I was running as hard as I could because I knew that Pete would be trying to pass me. And that's an image that can frighten the daylights out of you: Peter Snell swinging wide and charging down the track. Well sure enough, rounding the final turn I heard the crowd begin to roar. *Oh, boy,* I thought, *Pete's winding up his finishing kick.* So what did I do? I took a quick peek to my right just to check on things, and there he was, breathing down my neck. And right away I knew that I had a battle on my hands. As we turned into the homestretch we were side by side; I was giving it heaps to try to hold him off. But he wouldn't relent. That was Pete, eh? Such a champion; he never gave up. Anyway, with about 50 yards to go we were still shoulder to shoulder and I remember thinking that I might just sneak past him at the line. But somehow he was able to surge on in the final few yards and edge past me for the win.

Wow, very dramatic. What was your reaction afterward?

Well almost immediately I heard that I had broken four minutes, and I was dead chuffed about that. So I forgot almost straightaway that I had lost the race. Instead I was thinking how happy my parents would be for me, because I knew they were at home listening to the race on the radio. In those days, too, breaking four minutes was a huge step in your career. It meant instant credibility and respect around the track world. Within a week I began receiving invitations to compete here, there, and everywhere. It was also something for two New Zealanders to break four minutes in the same race. That was the first time that had happened. As a matter of fact, a lot of people thought it was wonderful that Pete and I had turned on such a great display for the queen. But I can assure you, Jim, pleasing the queen wasn't in either of our minds. We were just out there having a great race.

Did you get to meet the queen after all?

No. I think she had a few other things to attend to that day besides meeting me.

Now you just said, John, that breaking four minutes enhanced your reputation on the overseas running market, but did it change the way you thought about yourself as a runner?

I wouldn't say it did. I was just a keen athlete, after all, and happy to have run well. Honestly, I, didn't look at track or my identity as a runner any differently at all.

You didn't become more determined to beat Peter the next time, or to be sure you were ready for the Olympics the following year?

Jim, I wasn't that kind of athlete. I tended to live from race to race. For example, I never had long-term goals like getting to the Olympics. I gave more thought to the people I wanted to race, not the competitions I wanted to be in. Training was such a pleasure for me, too. It was something I really, really enjoyed, perhaps even more than racing. So I wouldn't say that I was ever that overly concerned about my future in athletics.

Was there anything you were concerned about as a runner?

Maybe nature. Maybe running in the forest and paying attention to the smells, the stillness, the quiet, and the birds. That used to overwhelm me at times, the peacefulness and beauty of the forest. And running with style was important to me, too. I was always conscious of the fact that I was taking part in something much bigger than me. In that sense, I would never just flop down the road. I believed I was participating in an art, if you like . . . and interacting with my surroundings. Because if you run every day of your life like I did as a serious sportsman, you have a training routine that usually begins and ends at the same time every day. And as the year goes by you notice changes in the weather, and changes in the light: the sun setting slightly earlier than the week before as you enter winter, and the days lengthening as you enter summer. Those were the sorts of things I was aware of as a runner. My interaction with the wider world around me.

That's quite a unique approach, John, this holistic attitude to running. Was that something Lydiard promoted?

Funny that, because my dear mentor Murray actually used to say to me, "John, do you know why I run? I run because I enjoy beating other people." And I used to think, *I should be more like that.* But I couldn't. That hot fire in your belly to beat the other guy wasn't me. And I used to feel terrible about that because I'd enjoy a race even if I lost. Like that one against Peter where I ran my first sub-four: That was just great fun. And I was so happy to have given my all and done well; I didn't really care that Pete had beaten me.

So it was the taking part that mattered to you?

It was the taking part, that's exactly right. That was what I enjoyed about track. But do you want to hear something curious? I've done a fair bit of coaching in my day, including coaching guys and gals who were Olympic finalists. But I didn't always share with them my thoughts about the importance of taking part versus winning. I'd say to them, for example, "You must have a plan for every race. You must run to win." Strange, eh, because that certainly wasn't what I ran for.

Photo by Ed Lacey

# America's Miler

## JIM RYUN
### (United States)

**First Sub-4: June 5, 1964, 3:59.0, Los Angeles**
**Personal best: 3:51.1**
**Total Sub-4s: 29**

*H*e *knows never to look over his shoulder, not even for a quick glance behind. The break in stride, the loss of momentum . . . it's simply bad tactics, and probably costs half a second or more. Besides, why give the others the satisfaction? The racing's ahead, not behind; that's where the real challenge lies . . . in the future, not the past.*

*But the past can sometimes be hard to ignore. In Jim Ryun's case especially: two mile world records, an Olympic silver medal, and iconic status as a 1960s boy wonder miler, the first American high schooler to run a sub-four-minute mile. That's enough security to last anyone a lifetime. But who wants to spend all of his time remembering the past? Certainly not Jim Ryun. Which probably explains why it's Congressman Ryun today, a third term representative from Kansas's second district, a site not too far from the very streets and fields where his running career began.*

*Our conversation took place on the floor of the House of Representatives. We spoke intermittently, during breaks in voting. I was in my flat in England, 10 o'clock on a Wednesday evening; he was on his mobile phone five hours earlier in Washington, D.C.*

*In all, our talk moved in this and that direction. Backward, too, as this miling legend kindly gave me a minute of his time to reflect on his running career and his first four-minute mile as a 17-year-old boy.*

Congressman Ryun, in the early 1960s, when you were just beginning to run yourself, Americans dominated the mile with 6 men in the world's top 10. Were you aware of this, and was it something that inspired you to become a miler?

I have to say that I knew almost nothing about the larger running scene in America when I was in high school. Really, I only started to run because I wanted to make some athletic team. Much like it is today for many young boys and girls, sport enabled me to fit in and make friends. And the cross-country team at my high school was the only team I could make. I wasn't quite good enough at baseball or basketball, or the other popular team sports. And when the cross-country season ended and track season began, well, the mile was the longest distance available in those days. So in effect, my choice to become a miler was made for me.

Your beginnings as a cross-country runner and a miler weren't too auspicious, in that you lost all your early races, yet you continued to train and race very hard. Why?

You're absolutely right in saying that I didn't have the greatest start to my running career. The first workouts I did almost killed me; I barely made the B team in cross-country, and when I ran my first mile in practice my time was 5:38. But you have to keep in mind my initial objective. It wasn't to be a star runner, or go undefeated, or win the Kansas state championships. Those ambitions only came later. My early goals were much simpler: I wanted to continue improving, and I wanted to win a letterman's jacket. But as I did begin to improve . . . and improve . . . and improve, I realized quite quickly that there might be something very unusual or special about my ability.

I should say. In your first year of running you ran a 4:07 mile, which was a world best for 16-year-olds, and you won the Kansas state championships. How did it feel to be so good at such a young age?

It was so many things: surprising, magical, extraordinary. I remember I ran 4:32 in what I would consider the first "real" mile race of my career, in March 1963, when I was 15. I followed that with miles in 4:26, 4:21, 4:19, 4:16, 4:08, and then that 4:07 you already mentioned. But when you start something new, like running was for me as a boy, there's a certain extent to which you can't appreciate what's going on and what your results mean. It's impossible to comprehend the uniqueness of what you're achieving when you're actually in the process of doing it.

So your rapid improvement was somewhat mysterious to you?

Yes, in a way. And there were times actually when I used to pinch myself and say, *Is all of this really happening to me?*

Do you remember there being a clear moment when you realized, *My God, this is happening to me?*

Probably as more and more magazine stories and newspaper articles were written about me. That had the effect of convincing me more than anything else that something pretty special was occurring. Because it's one thing to read this or that in a magazine or book, but when you are the subject of the magazine or book, that has a totally different effect.

Did you enjoy the astonishment your improvement brought to people?

Yes, because many people in the track world thought I was a flash in the pan. So it was nice to prove that my times were genuine, and to show them that I could hold my own against more senior runners. For example, I was very satisfied at the end of my junior year, in 1964, when I ran the California Relays against all the best milers in America and finished third in 4:01. My coach, in fact, nearly fell out of his seat after that result.

How difficult was it as a teenager to race against older, fully mature athletes?

Emotionally it wasn't that hard because the pressure to perform was on them more than me. But the races themselves were a challenge. Against runners my own age I felt I had an overwhelming advantage. While I still respected my high school opponents, I didn't need to do anything too special to win. But thankfully I developed a very potent kick toward the end of my junior year. I'm not sure how or where that came from, but I was glad to have it for those senior races I ran. It gave me a useful tactic, sprinting hard over the last half lap. In that 4:01 race, for example, I ran my last lap in 55 seconds, whereas off exactly the same pace a few weeks earlier at the state championships, I could only manage 60 seconds for my last lap. But it still took time for me to appreciate my various strengths and weaknesses, as well as the strengths and weaknesses of my competitors. I was learning every minute how to race and how to win. And running against older, stronger, and more experienced runners was vital to that process.

Were you also learning about the history of the mile and the tradition of four minutes as a magical barrier?

Oh, very much so. Like I said to you earlier, when I first began to run I wasn't aware of any sort of running culture or history. But that changed quite quickly as I became a stronger runner. On the West Coast there were these big mile invitationals that were shown on television. There was a phenomenal interest in the mile across America at that time. I remember one of the first races I watched involved Peter Snell from New Zealand. Wow, did he impress me as a great miler. I was also gathering any information I could find about running. One early book I read was the biography of Emil Zatopeck, and his fantastic achievements at the 1952 Olympics. And there were so many other books and stories I read.

What were you hoping to take from these stories on running, and from the mile races you watched on television?

I suppose I wanted to understand something about success, and how to achieve it. I wanted to know how to appreciate what was happening to me. So in their own way, those books I read and the races I watched on television became guiding lights to me for the future.

Why do you think the mile was so popular back in the 1960s?

The mile was the race of choice back then, and everyone could relate to it. People drove a mile to the store, or walked a mile somewhere. And most Americans were challenged at some point in their lives to think about running a mile. So it became a benchmark, a standard people identified with. I think it's terrible today that we don't run the mile and instead favor the 1500 meters. For an American audience the 1500 will never gain the same popularity or acceptance as the mile.

Was there ever a time in your career when you thought you might wake up one morning to find your talent gone?

No, that wasn't something I worried about. To be honest, I found it more daunting to come to terms with my future. For example, was running going to be part of my life for a very long time, or was it just some temporary phase?

Was Roger Bannister another famous miler you were aware of as a young runner?

When my high school coach, Bob Timmons, began programming me to think about becoming the first high school boy to run under four minutes, he told me about Roger Bannister and what he had done to achieve his epic feat of running the first four-minute mile.

Would you compare your achievement of becoming the first high school runner to break four minutes for a mile with Roger Bannister's achievement of becoming the first person to run under four minutes?

Only in the sense that they were both barriers that many people thought to be impossible.

Could you have broken four minutes as a schoolboy without the help of Coach Timmons, who as you just said programmed you to do it?

I don't think so. Because while I was fortunate enough to have an enormous amount of potential and God-given talent, I needed to be inspired as well. I needed someone who could nurture my talent and bring it along. And Coach Timmons played that part. He was a true visionary. As early as my sophomore year he began to talk to me about running under four minutes, and that was only after the fourth mile I had ever run. That was how far ahead he looked.

What exactly do you think he saw in you?

I think that I was willing to work very, very hard, which I was.

When he first spoke to you about becoming the first high school runner to break four minutes for a mile, did you understand what he meant?

No, I couldn't comprehend it at all. And I had no idea what four minutes signified, or whether it was something I could possibly achieve.

Would you say that having you run under four minutes was more Coach Timmons's goal than your own goal?

To a degree, I would. For example, there was never a moment when I was supremely confident that I could break four minutes. It didn't become a reality for me, or something that I believed was possible, until the night I actually did it.

Even though you had run 4:06 and 4:01 so easily, and you were showing no signs of slowing down?

You have to remember, Jim, I was only in my third year of running when I ran those times. I wasn't experienced enough to reflect on any of it. It was more Coach Timmons who was trying to plan and control everything. So sure, four minutes was a goal of mine, and yes I wrote it down on a piece of paper as something I hoped to achieve by my senior year, but a lot of that was purely out of respect for Coach Timmons and my acceptance of what he thought I was capable of doing. I was listening to him talk about four minutes all the time, and I was thinking about it more and more myself, but was it something I totally believed in? I'm afraid I can't say it was. At least not until I did it. Essentially, Coach Timmons had the very hard task of getting me to think beyond what I was experiencing, because four minutes was something unknown to me. And that's the hardest part of improving in any field or endeavor: believing you're capable of doing something that you have no knowledge or experience of. That's the hurdle you have to scale when you face a barrier, and there's usually never a map to show you the way. Which means finding out how to do it yourself.

Did Coach Timmons design specific workouts to strengthen your faith in breaking four minutes?

We were constantly trying innovative things in practice. We did lots of simulations to try to duplicate the feelings, sensations, and challenge of four minutes. For example, I might run a hard three-quarters and rest a minute and then run an all-out quarter. Everything we did in practice was to get me to believe that breaking four minutes was possible. And I have to say, those workouts were incredibly intense, and probably far beyond what was necessary to be a miler. We covered 10 to 15 miles in some interval workouts. And sometimes I'd come home from practice so tired and sick that I couldn't eat. But the mistakes we made were because we were new at what we were doing; we didn't realize that maybe we were pushing it too hard. When I think about it now, and the volume of work we did, and particularly the rapid buildup from zero training to full-time training, it's a miracle that I didn't get seriously injured in my first three years of running.

Did Coach Timmons treat you differently than the other runners on your high school team?

He really didn't, and that's because he made four minutes a goal for all of us. He wouldn't just talk to me about running under four minutes, he would talk to the entire team. He'd explain the historic nature of the four-minute mile, and how difficult it would be, and that we all had to believe and pray for it to become possible. And that made the training easier for me, because I felt like I had all my teammates' support. Coach Timmons would even design workouts for my teammates that could be used to pace or push me through my workouts. And that was a tremendous help.

What would you say was your greatest attribute as a miler?

I'm not sure. That's something I've never thought about before.

Would you say it was your ability to survive the punishing workouts Coach Timmons prescribed?

Yes, that was important. But harder than surviving any of his workouts was surviving the public's and the media's expectations. After all, those pressures were constant, whereas the pain associated with running was always temporary. For example, after my first year everyone was saying, *He's had a phenomenal beginning but he'll never continue to develop.* Then after I broke four minutes it was, *He's peaked too soon, he'll never continue to develop.* And after my first world record people were saying, *Well, this is great stuff but no way can it continue.* And on and on it went.

Why do you think people were so negative?

I'm not sure they were negative so much as unrealistic or naive about running. Just because I ran under four minutes once didn't mean I was going to run under four minutes in all my races. So if I ran 4:10, it didn't mean I was washed up. But that was how the press and the public usually saw it. All the same, those comments still really hurt me, and they took getting used to. It was only through the grace of God and the love and support of my family, Coach Timmons, and later my wife that I learned to ignore what other people said about me—people who, quite frankly, didn't understand what we were trying to achieve and what my abilities and talents were.

In talking about the difficulty of training, you once said, "You get used to the pain." What did you mean by that?

Running well entails a degree of desensitization, and going through a process whereby you accept the pain that's necessary to run fast. I have always maintained to a certain extent that an individual's ability to withstand the pressure of running and the pain of running will ultimately determine how fast he's going to run. If a person doesn't have a tolerance for pain, his chances of running fast become slimmer all the time. So if you go into a training session thinking, *Oh, man, this is going to be very painful,* you're not going to have a very good workout.

What did you used to think about going into a hard workout?

I simply accepted that what I was about to do was necessary if I wanted to achieve my goals.

And during a race, what would you think about then?

In races I would concentrate on my pacing and the different individuals I had to beat. Like the first time I raced Kip Keino, the only thing on my mind was beating him. I never really payed close attention to how I was feeling in races, or whether the effort I was exerting was easy or difficult. Basically, I subjected my body through the training I did to handle what I wanted to achieve in a race. And as the season would go on, and there would be more significant races to run, I'd concentrate more and more on developing my confidence and the appropriate running rhythm that would allow me to expect and produce good times.

Did you have a particular race strategy you favored?

I tended to favor staying with a reasonably good pace all the way through three-quarters and then accelerating with 300 or 200 yards remaining. When I crossed the finish line I wanted to feel as if I had nothing left, and that I had left my best race on the track. That was what gave me the most satisfaction.

Was your desensitization to pain something Coach Timmons instilled in you?

Yes, because he didn't accept complaining about the pain of running as any sort of excuse for not running your best either in a workout or in a race.

Pain's a natural part of being a runner, he felt, so there's no choice in the matter. You either learn to deal with it or quit. He used to say to us all the time, "It's not that you have to do these workouts, but that you get to do them." So his attitude and approach to running was quite hard, but if I hadn't been conditioned to think that way, I'm sure I never would have developed the resolve to break four minutes as a high schooler.

What can you tell me about your first time under four minutes? Because it was a very tactical race, wasn't it, with a lot of jostling and bumping, and in the end eight guys broke four minutes, four of them for the first time, which must have been remarkable back then?

It was one of those West Coast mile races I told you about, the Compton Invitational. And I was invited on the strength of my 4:01 two weeks earlier in Modesto. So along with Dyrol Burleson, Jim Grelle, and the other top American milers, I lined up for what was supposed to be a very fast race. Now, as you probably know, I have a partial loss of hearing in one ear, and as a result a partial loss of equilibrium, and at the 600-yard mark I got bumped quite hard and had to step off the track, which really disrupted my focus and rhythm. For a moment my confidence totally deflated. But that disruption also forced me to confront a fundamental question, *Was I going to get back on the track and do my best to be a player in this race, or was I simply going to go through the motions?* And because we had done so much work to get to that point, and because I believed it was time for me to see what I could really do, I decided to work my way back up to the front. So after working hard, and working hard, and working hard, I reached the front with just 200 yards to go.

And how did you feel then?

Very tired.

Well, you were only 17 after all, running against grown men.

I know, and I needed some time to recover after making up all that lost ground . . .

But it was time to kick?

It was, and I just didn't have anything left. And when they began to accelerate, I could only watch them pull away.

So the last straightaway was a struggle?

It was, and a bunch of guys passed me. When I crossed the finish line I was very disappointed. I felt that I had let everyone down by not positioning myself closer to the front for the final sprint. Then things became very confusing as we tried to figure out exactly how many runners had broken four minutes. Was it eight, and if so was I eighth or ninth? Nobody knew at first. Finally, the announcement came over the PA and confirmed what we suspected, I had finished eighth in 3:59.0, thus becoming the first high school runner to break four minutes for a mile.

Do you remember your reaction to that news?

I was excited, of course, but also relieved. I was also exhausted and kind of numbed by the whole thing. Breaking four minutes had been such an all-consuming goal in my life that when I realized I had done it I was faced with the question, *What do I do next?* Suddenly there was a void regarding my future. Was I going to try out for the Olympics, which were only a few months away? Or was I going to take a break? Later, though, the impact of it all did hit me, and I was very proud of what I had done. But the biggest effect breaking four minutes for the first time had on me was a shift in confidence. I began to believe in myself and my ability much more, and in Coach Timmons, too. I also realized that there were other frontiers for me to explore as a runner, international competition, world records, major championships, so instead of ending, my running life was actually just beginning.

# Heart of a Miler

## PEKKA VASALA
### (Finland)

**First sub-4: July 5, 1972, 3:57.2, Stockholm**
**Personal Best: 3:57.13**
**Total sub-4s: 5**

*S*ummer *in Finland presents spectacular shades of color: the blues of sky and lake water, the greens of pine and fir. The landscape is soft, quiet, and enduring as the sun's rays touch the other side of midnight. A Finnish summer provides a well-deserved exit to cold and darkness. As I have observed myself, winter here hangs low in the sky, a shoulder-level sun. The black ice is invisible, streetlights glow orange late into morning, and layers of grayness extend into people's lives. To say summer is rejuvenation and rebirth smacks of cliché, but to be here now in July, where folk music accompanies lakeside picnics and children's games, truly convinces me of the primacy of heat and sun to invigorate the soul.*

*Far and away nothing comforts the runner more than wood-chipped forest paths, or pine-needle trails. They cushion the bones and soften the endless miles logged. Increases in volume and intensity are absorbed painlessly, like padded gloves or an insulated jacket. Finnish runners glide through the woods like summertime skiers, ducking and wind-*

*ing beneath bended bows, and darting over rocks and roots. The forest is their sanctuary, not a dark dwelling to fear. It's where all Finnish runners consider who they are and re-establish their connection to home. First there was Paavo Nurmi, maybe the greatest athlete ever, the mile world-record holder and nine-time Olympic champion. And the names of his fellow Olympic champions, so exotic looking and difficult to pronounce, wrap this secluded land and its distance runners in mystery: Johannes Kolehmainen, Lauri Lehtinen, Ville Ritola, Ilmari Salminen, Toivo Loukola, Lasse Viren, and Pekka Vasala. They are sport woodsmen whose tracks are firmly layed in time.*

Pekka, because the mile run is not a "true" European event, did contesting it ever feel less serious to you than running, say, the 1500 meters?

It's true the 1500 meters was my main event because here in Finland we have the metric system; we were not raised on yards. When I competed at 1500 meters I was always very concerned about my place, world rankings, and being sure to win. This was the event the Finnish people would use to judge me. Yes, running a mile did sometimes feel like an exhibition, almost like I was running for fun with no pressure. I think that is one reason why I was okay to run the mile. To have a break from 1500 meters.

So the mile wasn't a "real" race for you?

No, no, no. I still wanted to win when I ran a mile. I always wanted to win when I stepped on the track.

Were you aware of the four-minute-mile standard?

Always, because Roger Bannister is a name every Finnish runner knows. This was a limit we respected, even though we seldom ran the mile. In Finland we appreciate history and tradition and our greatest runner ever, Paavo Nurmi, ran the mile. He was successful and a world-record holder; we always pay close attention to the mile and how it develops and changes. I also learned from Bannister's coach, Franz Stampfl, that what is the most important workout to do to prepare for a mile is 10 repetitions of 400 meters with a one minute rest. It was Bannister's training to get ready for his first four-minute mile.

Apparently, Bannister did his 10 just under 60 seconds each before his record run. What could you do for that workout?

I did 10 in fifty-seven seconds. I knew then I was ready to run fast and beat maybe anyone. It was my benchmark, that workout.

Can you remember the first mile you ever ran?

Oh, that's so many years ago now, but I think it was a small meeting in the west of Finland. I was such a young man then. I do know my time was 4:16. Then later, perhaps the next year, I ran 4:09. To improve always made me happy. I liked very much to be running faster times.

Is a four-minute mile still a standard that Finnish runners appreciate today?

I think so, yes. Of course the world record is so much better . . . what is it, seventeen seconds [under four minutes]? But for example, my son is 18 and a 1500-meter runner and he has run 3:43 this summer, which is almost equivalent to a four-minute mile. But he tells me he would also like to break four minutes for real.

Did he say why?

He thinks it means—and he is correct, I agree—that he becomes a good runner in the English way when he can break four minutes for a mile. I think so, also, because it's a standard that others outside Finland and Europe know, like in America. The New Zealander John Walker, he made the mile very known here in Scandinavia when he ran the first sub-3:50 mile in Sweden in 1975. Again, all Finnish runners, even normal Finnish people, know John Walker and his famous race in Sweden.

The Bislett Games in Oslo is perhaps the most important track meet of the year, and they continue to hold a mile. Do you think there is some particular romance between Scandinavians and the mile?

It's just my opinion, but I think so that the mile is imported to us because of the Englishmen Sebastian Coe, Steve Ovett, and Steve Cram. It's not natural for us today, the mile, but a result of these guys. They were great English runners and the mile was important to them. Our meetings in Scandinavia, like the Bislett Games, have the best atmosphere in the world, with the stands so near to the track where the athletes run and the people are loud and screaming and banging their feet. These Englishmen, they naturally want to race here and use our support to break records and times that matter to them, like the mile. And we are happy to help and just see fast times and new records. So the mile becomes important to us through them. At least maybe; this is what I think.

So for Scandinavian track fans it doesn't matter whether someone runs a world record over 1500 meters or the mile?

Not so much. They like any world record, and they understand the mile. It's simple, just four laps of the track. Any result that is new and better is good. Also, close races are good, and Coe, Ovett, and Cram made running very interesting and exciting with good rivalries.

So maybe it's people and their personalities that make sport interesting, not the event itself?

I think it's always people and their contests and their stories and where they are from that make sport interesting. Who wants to watch a nameless and faceless man run by himself?

But that almost seems to be the case today with every race loaded with rabbits and pacesetters to ensure a fast time.

I never thought about times, anyway. I was a competitor and racer. I never ran for time, just winning. In my day we had no rabbits so I didn't think so much about the time.

How fast do you think you could have run a mile using a rabbit?

That's easy, under 3:50 for sure.

That would have made you the world-record holder in 1972.

Yes, it was possible.

So you would have been as happy to have broken the mile world record as you would have the 1500 world record?

Sure, sure, sure. All the world records are important; all world records are difficult. If I could have held any one of them, even something like the 2000 meters or 2 miles, I would have been very pleased.

Do you think it's possible, Pekka, that because there are no world-class English milers today, the mile might have trouble surviving as a popular sporting event and perhaps fall off the program at meetings like the Bislett Games?

That's a difficult question. Maybe for less elite middle-distance runners, at least in Europe, they won't care about the mile because they always need a better and better 1500 time to qualify for more important meetings and championships. But as long as there is money for new records, the very top guys will keep running the mile because it's another race they can be the best at. Not just that, I think even the African runners want to belong to the same history of mile world-record holders like Bannister, Peter Snell, and Jim Ryun. At least that is what El Guerrouj said after he broke the mile world record last in Rome two years ago.

Can we talk about your first sub-four-minute mile?

Sure. It was in Stockholm in July 1972. I ran easily and it was just before the Munich Olympics so I was in top shape.

Did breaking four minutes so easily boost your confidence going into the Olympics?

Yes, it was an important time of year to run fast and prove my fitness before the Olympic Games. Also, I had done badly in the years before the Olympics—for example, 1971, in the European championships—so the Finnish people did not expect much from me at Munich. I had no pressure at the Olympic Games, but inside I felt like I was a strong favorite because I was feeling so good in my races leading up to the Olympics, like in Stockholm when I ran that mile.

How did the race in Stockholm go?

I beat an Englishman after sitting behind him most of the way. I kicked very hard the last 200 meters.

Were you thinking about your time and whether you were close to four minutes?

Like I said before, I never thought about time. But I was very pleased when I heard 3:57. It was like a double victory. The first victory was winning the race and the second victory was breaking four minutes.

What do you think about all the recent changes in running? The money, sponsorship, television . . .

I could be rich today if I was running; to have money, though, is not the only happiness. But that is old history, my running career. It's past. I need to leave it behind—otherwise I have no chance to become someone else in my life. Here in Finland it's a small country, and people are crazy about track and field. I have to be careful not to talk about my running because then the people don't let me change. That is why this interview is something rare . . . I never talk about my running, not even to my son unless he asks me. For many years after I stopped running in 1972, people would come up to me and say, "Oh, you are the runner." This I didn't like, because I was not a runner anymore. But I understand how people are. They are so keen about sport and they want us in Finland to be great in track and field, especially our tradition in the distance events. But I was retired and trying to become a businessman. So today it makes me happy when I can speak to someone about business and he never mentions my running. It makes me think that I have done well in business. Also, I think we were better runners than they are today. So many athletes in Finland are more sport tourists. They are satisfied with less. For example, they are usually just happy to be named to the Olympic team. Then they stop thinking about getting better or trying to win. We were always very eager to win races. Today they make a qualifying standard and they stop trying.

Could that be because more kids ran when you were a boy and the internal competition was greater?

True, today there are so many more choices for young people like television, computers, video games, music. But I think we also had more pure aspirations for enjoying running, like being in the forest, or exercising alone with our thoughts and feeling good. Today there is so much science and special coaching and worrying about times. And a lot of what these coaches say is wrong. But mainly they don't run enough today. I watch my son and he runs half as much in a week as I did.

How much did you run a week?

More than 200 kilometers.

That is a lot.

Okay, but it's not so hard to be a great runner. You just keep running more and more.

Yes, but surely one also needs some talent or at least a disposition to be a runner?

We were more simple as runners, and maybe that's better. I don't know, I am not a sport philosopher, but as a boy I loved all sports, especially cross-country skiing and ice hockey. I was always outdoors or in nature. It was how I spent my free time, in the fields. It was our way for fun. And when my stamina improved and running became easier, it gave me great power and strength. That was so enjoyable.

Was racing also enjoyable for you?

Racing, you were like an actor. You make a show for a crowd and ought to do your best to win. In this way, the warm-up became exciting for me and the nerves gave me tingling and adrenaline. You have to concentrate through all of this to bring everything out of your body. Racing is the most important. There is no reason to train if you don't race.

So what do you miss more today, training or racing?

I don't miss racing at all. But I'm missing being in good shape and not so heavy. The feeling that you can run forever like an animal is very special. It gives you freedom, that: to be light, fast, and strong. Especially to be running in the forest among nature where you can see the landscape. I would like to be alone and calm running through the forest again. To smell different trees and grass, to hear the birds, to see the wild animals would be very nice. That's why I still enjoy cross-country skiing today. It keeps me out in the forest. And there is no pain in skiing, either. It's smooth and easy and good exercise for a fat old man like me. But still nothing is the same for a runner as running.

As a boy did you always want to be a runner?

I wanted to play ice hockey for Finland. That is how most Finnish boys think. Hockey is our most important sport. But when I was young a puck crushed my chin. It was so painful and I had many days afterward suffering in the hospital. I didn't like that at all. I decided to give up hockey and start running because it was easy for me. At the first race at school I beat all the boys.

Did middle-distance events like the mile appeal more to you than the 5K and 10K, which were the real traditional events for Finnish runners?

To begin to answer that question I have to say that I am a lazy man and didn't want to run so many miles in training to be a top long-distance runner. Also, I am tall (6-foot-3) and so I thought the mile was better for my long legs. Plus, I had a strong 800-meter time, 1:44, so I had speed to be a miler. This was good news to me not to have to run the 5K. Also, the Finnish distance runners—even though we had so many great ones, like Nurmi, Kolehmainen, Lehtinen, and Ritola—were not my real heroes. Herbert Elliott from Australia was my hero. I looked at him winning the 1500 meters in the Rome Olympics in 1960 and I started thinking about being an Olympic champion. I can remember his race because one man in our neighborhood bought a television to watch the Olympic Games and all the boys were in his living room watching, too. Also in Rome, Peter Snell, the New Zealander, won the 800 meters and afterward I was copying his style for many years where I kept my arms low down by my side.

But certainly the legendary Finnish runners must have inspired you to work hard and be part of that tradition?

Well, you can say that, yes, I wanted to be part of that same kind of history as Paavo Nurmi, but it was not the leading point for me. I think the most important thing for me was I was curious how fast I am capable of running and how good can I be. So when I won the gold medal in Munich and became Olympic champion I had enough because that is the top and it is not so easy to practice the amateur way. At that time, you have to remember, I was not a full-time runner. There were only under-the-table payments, and they were not enough. Had I been a runner today I would have kept running so long time because it is possible to make a very good living.

You said before that you thought you had a good body for the mile, tall and long legs, what about your mind—was it good for the mile?

I suppose it must because I was Olympic champion. But what I can say is that I have good concentration skills. For three or four minutes I can be very intense and focused . . . I can be patient. I was not an aggressive runner, but a patient runner with a kick. This is also being smart, and as Finns we are careful about not saying or doing something that we can't know about. We are happy to watch and wait. So being a Finn also shaped how I ran races. And I ran many races to learn smart tactics. I lost many races, too, but always

I was learning about new ways of winning. Today milers have bad tactics because of the rabbits in all their races; they never learn how to race the way we did. The Olympics is a different type of competition than a Grand Prix meeting and aiming for a world record. A world record doesn't matter in the Olympics, the place across the finish line does; that must be what you care about most.

What else did you care about as a runner? For example, did you have any superstitions or good-luck charms that you believed helped you?

Only one thing: a necklace of a heart that my wife gave me. I always raced with that and so with her love. I guess you can say in your book that I ran for love and with love.

Photo: Colour Sport

# Tracking a Force

## JOHN WALKER
### (New Zealand)

**First sub-4: July 7, 1973, 3:58.8, Victoria, Canada**
**Personal best: 3:49.08**
**Total sub-4s: 127**

*The smell of leather hits me first . . . rich, deep, luxurious. Then an imposing figure in conversation on the phone, burly almost, gestures me farther inside. The gleaming equipment, the range of accoutrements—it's like some imperial hardware store. Clearly, this man has moved on in life; evident from these surroundings is his ability to pursue other interests with equal intensity, professionalism, and seriousness. John Walker was a lion on the track. For his longevity and ferocity as a competitor he stands alone.*

*His phone conversation continues, questions accented by more questions. All of which gives me more time to browse. Saddles imported from Italy, stirrups by way of England, and tailored French chaps. Tack, I soon learn, is what all this equipment is called. He was bronzed and rugged in his prime. Barrel-chested and kitted out in black with beads and long hair flowing; he was a wonder—mile world-record holder, Olympic*

*1500-meter champion. And he obviously still possesses the will to lead a triumphant life today.*

*John Walker remains a New Zealand icon. His equestrian supplies shop which borders an eastern ridge of open fields and new housing developments on the outskirts of Auckland, is his present obsession. He is the last link in an impressive line of world-beating male distance runners this tiny island nation has produced. Today's visitor to New Zealand expects beaches, Maori song, and expansive green spaces. Like everywhere in the world, sport in this society has changed. Runners here train and compete anonymously now. Unlike the life and times of the once and future King of the Mile.*

John, how relevant or significant is the mile run today?

Let me just start off by saying this. The mile is without question the most significant event in track and field. And I say that unreservedly, not just because I ran the mile. Everyone can relate to four times around a track at 60 seconds per lap. In two decades as a world-class runner, I saw no event capture the imagination and enthusiasm of a crowd like the mile. That's just a fact. And may I add to that by saying, the mile is also the hardest event to run. And again, I think I can say that unreservedly because I ran them all, from the 5000 to the half marathon.

What do you think makes the mile so difficult?

It's the most complex to train for because of the mix of speed and strength that's needed, and it's the hardest to race because you have to be alert and conscious of ever-changing tactics. It's a true thinking man's race. In that regard, it calls for the complete runner. And add to that, its mythical nature. It's simple and pure; almost magical, I'd say. And it will be around forever. For example, it's still every boy's dream who becomes a middle distance runner to run a sub-four-minute mile.

You think so, even though times today are so much faster?

Yes, I do. And times are faster, that's true. But the mile has history and tradition on its side, particularly a four-minute mile. People naturally strive to succeed and achieve standards that are respected and appreciated. As one of sport's ultimate challenges, the prestige of running a four-minute mile can only survive. Look at my career. I have run well over 100 sub-four-minute miles, yet I still regard my first one as a landmark. Young runners today are looking for some confirmation of their talent and ability, and running under four minutes provides that more than anything else.

When did the dream of breaking four minutes emerge for you?

Not until I was 20. But that's not because I was a late bloomer. Up until 17 my main sport was tennis. Although I ran cross-country in the winter, I never ran track because I was playing tennis all summer. So the dream of a four-minute mile was never a real one for me, even though I was a huge athletics fan and admired the mile more than any other event. But because I didn't have the times on the track, I didn't believe that I was good enough to break four minutes. My best was only 4:06 through my teenage years. To be a sub-four-minute miler was something I definitely thought about and wanted to achieve, but I never imagined I could do it. It was more of a surprise, actually, my first sub-four-minute mile. It wasn't something I was planning or expecting. It happened almost by accident.

How was that?

I went to Canada when I was 20 to represent New Zealand in the 800 meters at the Pan Pacific Games. This was my first international race, and in fact my first time away from New Zealand. Rick Wohlhuter from the USA was running, and he was the 800 world-record holder. Of course, he won, but I managed to finish third and I was quite delighted to get my bronze medal. Well, I thought that was the end of our trip and that we would be going back home to New Zealand, but it emerged that there was a satellite meeting in Victoria, and for some reason I had been entered in the mile. But there were two sections of the mile that day. All the top guys were put into the A race, whereas because my best time was only 4:06, I had to run with the second-string runners in the B race. And I have to say that I was annoyed by that. After my third place behind Wohlhuter I thought I deserved to run with the best guys. I suppose I was already beginning to get a little cocky and arrogant. Anyway, I started the B race as scheduled, and led wire to wire and ran

3:58.8. That was my first sub-four-minute mile and, looking back on it now, probably the defining moment that kick-started my career.

Can you tell me more about the actual race—for example, your splits and your reaction to becoming a sub-four-miler?

There was no one decent in the race. I just ran hard from the front. Maybe some Canadian led off the line and around the first turn, but then I took control and ran even splits with a 58-second last lap. My philosophy then, as always, was to run to win. Only once or twice in my career did I deliberately go into a race thinking about time. My world record in Sweden in 1975, when I became the first runner to go beneath 3:50, was one occasion. Otherwise, I went into every race thinking about winning. Initially, of course, I was delighted to have broken four minutes, but when the A race was won in 3:57.9, I got very angry. I thought if they had let me run that race I would have won it.

Was there much reaction in New Zealand when the news came that you had broken four minutes?

It was headlines. In those days, running success was truly valued in New Zealand, not like today. And it was always big news when someone broke four minutes. At that time we had two great runners, Rod Dixon and Dick Quax, and lots of other guys around 4:01 or 4:02. I was seen as the new man on the scene, and in some ways expected to carry the flame after Dixon and Quax. So the reaction was quite positive, which boosted the way I thought about myself and my ability. I really began to think that I could achieve something in athletics.

So what came next for you?

When I got back to New Zealand I sold my car and headed straight to Europe to try to get into some better races. I was really excited to run faster, and I was looking for any opportunity at all. With help from Dixon and Quax I was able to get into some good races, and I managed to improve all my times that season and beat some pretty good runners. After that summer in

Europe following my first sub-four-minute mile, I was hooked into becoming a serious runner. I loved the whole lifestyle of traveling and competing. My career really began then.

Did you ever imagine at that point that you'd go on to break the mile world record just two years later?

Quietly, in the back of my mind I always believed that I was capable of reaching that sort of level. Even though my times as a teenager weren't so fast, I was improving every year, even if it was just by half a second. And that kept me thinking that anything was possible. I also knew that New Zealand runners didn't come right until 23 or 24. Because of all the cross-country training we do, our speed doesn't peak until later. In general, I'd say that we're a slow-maturing people. So entering my 20s I was fresh and feeling good. I wasn't burned out like so many Americans are who get used and discarded by the collegiate system. I was eager, enthusiastic, and committed. My coach Arch Jelly saw my potential, too. And in fact, he told me when I was a teenager that I'd be better than Peter Snell, that I'd rewrite the record books, that I'd be an Olympic champion, and that I'd be the first person to break 3:50 for the mile.

Did you believe him?

I thought he was mad. But honestly, he was a visionary, Arch was. For example, the night before the 1974 Commonwealth Games he told me that I'd break the world record for 1500 meters, which was five seconds below my best. And he was right. The only problem was that I lost the race to Filbert Bayi. What I am trying to say, though, is that Arch Jelly believed in me, and I believed in him, and really that was the basis of our relationship. Do you know that in 20 years of our working together he only missed one workout, and that was because his car broke down? That's how loyal he was. And I tried to repay that loyalty every day by running as hard as I could.

Who else besides Arch supported you as a young runner?

My biggest support came from my club mates. As a teenager I would get distracted very easily, and I loved to have late nights. Quite regularly I would stay out until 5 A.M. on a Saturday. But at 8 o'clock Sunday morning my club mates would come around to my house in their running gear, sometimes as many as 20 of them, to get me up for our regular Sunday 22-mile run. And they'd throw stones on our roof and knock on my window until I got out of bed. So I had no choice but to go running, even if I had had only two hours of sleep. Really, these were the guys who kept me running during those crucial formative years when I could have so easily been led astray. Left to my own devices, I'm sure that I never would have made it as a runner. Because training to me was such a chore, especially the long runs. I hated doing them the most. But here were all these dedicated club runners who loved going out for long runs dragging me along. It was some sight, those early mornings across Auckland back in the 1970s. There were huge packs of runners out on the hills on any Saturday or Sunday. That's gone today, of course, and explains why New Zealand is so poor in distance running. You need that thriving club culture to breed success and carry forward your nation's traditions; otherwise they'll just die.

In what way, then, did the tradition of New Zealand miling, from Jack Lovelock, who set the world record in 1933, to Peter Snell who set the record twice in the 1960s, inspire you?

I remember being in school on the day of Snell's 1500-meter race at the Tokyo Olympics, and sneaking out of the classroom to go into the bathroom with my transistor radio. It was terribly exciting to be cheering for this famous New Zealander beating the best in the world. But more exciting to me was Rod Dixon's 1500 bronze medal in the 1972 Olympics, which I stayed up until 2 A.M. to listen to live on the radio. It was at that time that I was beginning to formulate my own Olympic dreams, and Dixon was someone I knew, unlike Snell, so cheering for him had more immediacy and relevance to me. Do you know that as a nine-year-old boy I drew a picture of myself on a podium with a gold medal around my neck? The Olympics were a big motivation for me. And I remember being terribly upset when I learned that they didn't have cross-country in the Olympics because as a young boy I thought that was my best event. Through all of primary school I went undefeated in cross country. I even won races on the road. And I did all of that in bare feet with no real training.

So you were a natural?

I was. I was born with great stamina and strength. And I found those early cross-country events very easy. I'd just go to the front and wait until the last few meters and then sprint away for the win. In fact, I didn't lose a race until I was 17, when I went to a real track meet for the first time and had to compete against boys who were in full-time track training—whereas my only training had been to get from one place to another. I ran to and from school, which was 3 miles away. And I ran to and from tennis, which could have been up to 10 miles sometimes. I had no other choice because our family car was either always broken or Dad had to use it to go somewhere.

When did you give up tennis and begin to train more seriously as a runner?

That would have been when I was 18 or 19.

Was it a difficult decision?

Not so much. There were too many people telling me about my great potential as a runner. And to be honest, running was what I liked best and what I dreamed of doing and succeeding at. I knew the whole history of the mile, for example. I had read every book there was. Like Roger Bannister's, *The First Four Minutes,* and Murray Halberg's story. I must have read Peter Snell's book, *No Bugles, No Drums* 10 times. But still I never had that sub-four-minute-mile dream myself until later, when I was around 20.

When you prepared for a top mile race, did you have a favorite workout to gauge your readiness?

Yes, before important races I liked to do time trials by myself on the track. If I could run 5000 meters in training in 13:30, that was always a good indication to me that I was fit and strong. I also ran 1:45 for 800 meters in training one night. And I often broke four minutes in training. Once I ran 3:50.5 all by myself. I have to say that the key thing for me was always my strength. I ran my fastest times following a 100-mile week of training. I didn't need to do lots of short sprints to peak. Before my mile world record I ran two weeks of 100 miles without a single track workout. Whereas most guys would taper down before an important race, I'd do more hard mileage. That was what worked for me.

What did it mean to you to break the mile world record?

It was more significant to me than winning the Olympics. In many ways it was like a knighthood, that title. I feel it gave me an aura that command-ed respect wherever I went. More than anything else in my career, I loved being the mile world-record holder. It was a dream come true.

Would you say it changed you?

It changed me overnight. Up until that point in my life I always wondered what people had to do to become famous. What did it take, for example, to get your picture in a book, or for people to write stories about you? I had read so much about the great milers of the past, and I wanted to know what it took for that to happen . . . to be great. Well, I found out. It takes one race. That's what it takes. One performance in your life to lift you from obscurity. And my life changed within 10 minutes after that race. When I got back to the hotel with the other guys, we filled the bathtub with beer, which was a good Kiwi tradition, then the phone rang and I sat down to answer it, and there began 24 hours of interviews with press from all over the world, includ-ing *Time* and *Sports Illustrated*. Roger Bannister even called me, which was a tremendous honor, because here was this great miler whom I had held up as a god calling me, just a young Kiwi bloke. But you know, people say that my breaking 3:50 for the first time was comparable to his breaking four minutes for the first time, but I don't believe it. I think what he did was harder and more significant.

Why?

He had more psychological baggage and pressure to contend with. People thought it couldn't be done. Whereas sub-3:50 seemed to come along quite naturally . . . it was never this huge barrier. And Bannister had less competition, worse tracks, and stricter rules governing when you could race and where. That was a monumental effort for 1954. I mean, it's still an achievement today.

When you look back at that first sub-3:50, do you consider it the perfect race?

Far from it. The pacesetter did a terrible job. He ran 55 for the first lap and 60 for the next lap, which was a waste of energy. There was no competition in that race, either, and for the last lap and a half I was all by myself. If I had had some decent help with the pace that night, and a few people around to make things more competitive, I would have run 3:47. Another mistake I made was that I should have done it in America. If I had done it there, where the Americans are just crazy about sport and the mile in particular, I think I could've been financially secure for the rest of my life.

Speaking of finances, what do you think about all the money in track and field today?

It's not sour grapes, and you can never go back in time, but obviously I didn't make as much money running in my day as I could have made today. However, in saying that, the atmosphere of track was much better during my time. Today it's the agents who control everything, and the athletes are like zombies who just go out onto the track and perform. They have no rapport with the fans; they don't even know who the meet organizers are. Granted our conditions were terrible, and we had to stay five or six to a room, and we traveled by train, bus, and boat, and there were no doctors available for us. But I think we were tougher for it. We used to go to bars and discos after our races and drink until 3 A.M. We had parties all the time in our rooms. The athletes today don't do that. They have no sparkle, they're lifeless. And they'll realize once they're finished with their career that they may have made a lot of money, but that's all they have. Because at the end of the day you have to have memories, friends, and fun. That, in my mind, is the mark of a good career.

Did the world see the best of John Walker?

I don't believe so. For instance, I should have run fewer races and gone for more world records. Also, I lost 1977 to injury, which was really a prime time in my career. And during my era I really had no competition, which is no disrespect to the other athletes. But if you look over my results, I won hundreds of races by 20 or 30 meters. I didn't have anyone pushing me, and I didn't have the benefit of pacesetters like they do today. So I don't think I ever got the most out of myself. Unfortunately, when Coe, Ovett, and Scott came along I was past my prime. Had I had those guys on my heels I would have done something really fantastic. But in the end, it doesn't matter, because essentially I loved running the mile. I loved being such a dominant miler for so many years, which I believe I was. And throughout my career, no matter how small the event or the occasion, whenever I ran the mile I always set out to break four minutes. That, I think, is the defining statement on my career as a miler: 129 races below four minutes.

Photo by George Herringshaw

# A Winning Combination

## EAMONN COGHLAN
### (Ireland)

First sub-4: April 25, 1975, 3:56.2, Philadelphia
Personal best: 3:49.78
Total sub-4s: 78

*T*he *Golden Age of Miling, defined by most sport historians as the period following World War II when milers across Europe, Australia, and America approached and eventually surpassed four minutes, was typified by the gentleman-miler. Running was considered more avocation than profession, and Roger Bannister, who epitomized this era, represented Old World privilege and Oxford romanticism. His contemporaries were similarly placed: white, amateur, and of European descent.*

*The world of records is a restless business, however. The tallest tree grows higher, the widest river widens. And so it was that another mythical miling milestone arose in the wake of Bannister's first sub-four, a sub-3:50 mile.*

*It took 21 years following Bannister's first sub-four for a 3:49 mile to be run. This launched an unprecedented revitalization of the mile between 1975 and 1984. As in the early 1950s, crowds turned out in the ten of thousands to witness epic mile clashes between Sebastian Coe, Steve Ovett, John Walker, Steve Scott, and others. The number of new sub-four-minute milers in a single year (1982) reached 30 for the first time. Track invitationals in capital cities on five continents included the mile on their program. Born were the Golden Mile, the Dream Mile, and the Fifth Avenue Mile. Thirteen men ran below 3:50 for a mile 35 times between 1975 and 1984. The world record was lowered an unprecedented six times. Prize money soared, and television beamed live coverage of highly publicized mile matchups across the world. Furthermore, not a single performance from the 1960s and early 1970s remained on the mile's ever-expanding top 50 list. And nationalities represented in the mile's end-of-year top 10 rankings were more diverse than ever—New Zealand to Tanzania, Sudan to Spain, and Ireland to the United States. The mile truly became a global event. It was the Second Golden Age of Miling, where membership in the sub 3:50 club, like membership in the sub-four club 30 years earlier, became the true emblem of success. And in the heat of it all was an Irish miler named Eamonn Coghlan.*

Eamonn, do you remember when breaking four minutes for a mile first became a clear goal in your mind?

I do: September 1974, at the start of my sophomore year at Villanova.

Really, not until then?

That's because in high school in Ireland running for time was never so important. It was winning and losing that mattered. I was always taught to focus on winning . . . that the times will eventually come. To be honest, I can't even tell you my best times from high school . . . maybe around 4:10 for a mile, and 1:53 for a half-mile. My coach, Gerry Farnan, a great man, a wonderful man, influenced me in this regard. He said, "The more races you win, the faster you'll ultimately run." That sounded smart enough to me, so I never gave much thought to times after that.

So as a young runner, were you aware of Roger Bannister and the history and significance of the four-minute mile?

Oh, of course. My father had a huge interest in track and field. As a boy he was into running in a big way, and he was good enough all right on the local level. Anyway, he would tell me stories about the great milers like Roger

Bannister, Ron Delany, and Herb Elliott. At the cinema, too, they showed sport reports, or bits of sport news before the feature show. And always there was something to do with the mile. But it was mostly through my father that I came to understand athletics. He was passionate about running, and like a good Irishman full of great tales. Like Delany's 1500 gold medal in Melbourne in 1956, which apparently all of Ireland listened to live on the radio, or Elliott's 1958 mile world record right here in Dublin at Santry Stadium.

Was it his stories that inspired you to become a runner?

I have to say that it wasn't until 1964, when I was 11, and I joined the local athletics club in Dublin, that my genuine interest in running began. That was when I started my formal education, if you will, into the history of track and field. I was reading all sorts of books and magazines about running and coaching, and actively investigating different questions I had about who was who and so on. I also remember from a very young age going to see one particular cross-country race year after year. It was a 10 mile race held on St. Stephen's Day, or Boxing Day—December 26, the day after Christmas. All these runners slogging through the mud and muck amazed me; they were totally soaked and covered in dirt, which to me was just an incredible sight. I also went to Santry Stadium with my dad to see Peter Snell, Kip Keino, and the other great milers of the 1960s. But honestly, it wasn't until I began running myself, and then actually winning some races and feeling comfortable running, that my interest grew. And subsequently, because I knew the history of the mile from my father's stories, and the significance of four minutes, I did have a vision or dream quite early on of wanting to be a great miler myself, and maybe even breaking four minutes someday. Although this was a young boy's fantasy; at this point, four minutes hadn't become a real goal for me.

So when four minutes did become a real goal for you at Villanova your sophomore year, was your progress smooth?

I'll tell you about that, because looking back on the whole four-minute thing now it's quite interesting really. As a freshman at Villanova I ran lots of mile races indoors, outdoors, and on relays. And always I was around 4:01, or 4:02, which I can admit came quite easily for me. But at the start of my sophomore year, when I first thought I was ready to break four minutes, I decided that I needed some specific time to aim for. So what did I do? I took the mirror off the wall in my bedroom and on the back of it wrote down a time.

What did you write?

I wrote, 3:53.

Come on, 3:53, and you hadn't even broken four yet?

That's right. I hadn't even broken four minutes yet. But I was very determined at this point to be a good runner. You see, I hadn't trained very seriously up until then. But the summer between my freshman and sophomore year at Villanova, I ran the 5000 meters at the European championships in Rome. I spent a lot of time around great runners like Brendan Foster and Lasse Viren. And I was so inspired by these guys that I came away from those championships thinking, *Okay, Eamonn, it's time to get serious. If you want to be like them you have to start training like them.* And for the first time I began to do morning runs, I went to bed early, I ran on my own on Sundays, I started eating well, and I set time goals for myself, like that 3:53.

So you started to do all the necessary little things, whereas before would you say that running well just came naturally to you?

Yes, and I'd say running for me was naturally exhilarating, too. For example, I thoroughly enjoyed the feeling of speed. It was that simple . . . the pleasure of running fast . . . and of course winning.

And those feelings of exhilaration and enjoyment lasted throughout your career?

They did. I always loved the sensation of speed and fast running . . . Mind you, there were times when running was just hard work, too. For example, at the start of a season when I was getting back in shape, or when I was returning from an injury. I'd be out of breath straightaway and sore for days. It was awful. But once I was fit and things began to come easier, like the long runs and track intervals, that was when I could really concentrate on all the rich physical and mental sensations that running brought me.

Can you think of an example?

One was the disappearance of time. I could go running for well over an hour sometimes without any sense of how long I'd been gone. It wasn't so much that time sped up or slowed down, it just passed . . . It became something I stopped thinking about as I got deeper and deeper into the run, and deeper and deeper into myself. And there was always the sights and sound of nature surrounding me when I ran: hearing birds, taking in all the smells, seeing some wildlife, maybe. I loved that about running, being out in the countryside. But again, that was something I could only enjoy when I was in shape. Jumbo Elliott, my coach at Villanova, and another great man in my life, used to say to us, "I want you guys to run until you can smell the roses." In other words, until we were fit enough to enjoy our running and not treat it like a struggle.

Was running musical or rhythmical for you? For example, the idea of four laps in four minutes is a very even beat.

I couldn't stand to hear music in my ears when I ran. I could never run with a Walkman, for example. It would drive me nuts. I had to have that inner music playing in my head, that focus on my body and how I was feeling, reacting, and changing during the course of a workout. I wanted to enjoy the natural sensations or feedback I was getting out of being in shape and in control. That was music to me. That real feel-good sensation. And on an outdoor track running a mile, or doing repeat quarter miles in training, which I did hundreds and hundreds of, I had this 60-second rhythm in my head: 60, 60, 60. It was like a metronome; it became as natural a sound to me as my own breathing or my voice. And indoors, on an 11-laps-to-the-mile track, I had a 22-second rhythm in my head. Somehow I always thought about running in terms of sound, or pace; I was breaking down every stride into a cadence. Also, I would visualize my races when I was training, and that required concentration, sensitivity, and paying attention to myself, so again, the last thing I wanted was blaring music distracting me. Once in Madison Square Garden they brought in the Yale band to play the theme song to *Chariots of Fire* during the mile. God, I hated it. It was so slow, you know how it goes, da-da-da-da-da . . . that totally messed me up, although I did still manage to win the race.

You were known for having a great kick at the end of your races. What was the rhythm or sound you heard when you kicked?

My kick actually wasn't so much a sustained drive to the finish like most kicks are, but more of an acceleration, like changing gears. And I loved doing that, making a sudden move and passing by the field. Especially indoors where I could use the steep banks and the tight bends to ricochet off the turn. It gave me the most tremendous feeling of speed to drop down and shift like that . . . the feeling of centrifugal force as I whipped around. That acceleration reflex was totally embedded in my mind and body. I could do it at will almost, not just on the last lap but anytime during a race when I needed to get past someone or break out of a box.

Also the crowd, especially indoors, went crazy when you "made your move." Were you aware of that?

I always loved the interaction with the crowd. And indoors, because everything was so close and tight and packed in, it made me feel like I was part of what was happening—so involved, you know, not distant like in a big outdoor stadium. That meant racing indoors was more emotional for me, and those emotions, I have to say, were a terrific motivating factor.

With all the excitement you created at indoor track meets like the Milrose Games, did you ever think of yourself as a miler-showman?

No, because what mattered most to me was winning my races. That was always in the forefront of my mind whenever I stepped onto the track. Okay, I had decided that I didn't want to be a sports star who was considered aloof, and sure I was always conscious of the people and the crowd and the importance of recognizing them, but the bottom line was always winning. You could say that I simply wanted to give of myself . . . I appreciated people's support; after all, I'm a people person, so why not go with the people and be with them? To me that's a very different attitude from starting a race with the express purpose of pleasing or entertaining the crowd. For example, I worked extremely hard developing my kick—not to show off, but because I knew how effective it was at winning races. I did drills all the time to increase my reaction time. I could be out on an easy 10-miler, let's say, but still four or five times I'd drop gears, bang, and go. It was a way to keep refining my reflexes. You see, I wasn't really all that fast. My best 400 was only around 50 seconds, but I could turn that speed on quickly, within 2 or 3 yards if I had to.

Can you remember the first race you won using your kick?

Not so much my first win using my kick, but I do remember the first race I ever won. I was a boy, maybe only 12, and there was a 1-mile cross-country race down at the local athletics club. Before the start the coaches were telling me to take it easy and follow the older boys, some of whom were 18. But the gun went off and I just eased into the lead after a couple of hundred yards. And my goodness, were the lads behind me yelling. "Come on back. Get back here, Coghlan, you'll get lost." But I just looked over my shoulder and said to them, "No I won't, I'll follow the flags around. I'll just follow the flags." And I did, all the way to the finish line.

Speaking of your early experiences running, I'm interested in your life growing up in Dublin in the late 1950s. For example, what choices or options did you have in terms of playing sport?

Through school my choices were Gaelic football and hurling, and outside of school it was soccer. I played a lot of soccer, in fact, for a local Dublin club called Rialto. And for two years I was playing soccer and running. But at around 14 years of age I had to make a decision: *Do I run or do I play soccer?*

You couldn't carry on doing both?

I couldn't because the schedules for soccer games and athletics practice were beginning to overlap, and Gerry [Farnan], my athletics coach, was always telling my dad about my potential as a runner. I think Gerry and my dad deep down hoped that I'd get more serious about running. Because in those days I was what was known as a joiner. I started lots of things, but ended up quitting them all. Running was really the first activity that captured my attention. Besides, in running I was winning all my races and coming home every weekend with a medal, and sometimes two: one as an individual and another for the team. With soccer there was no hardware . . . we were never winning any medals. So I gave it up completely, and focused right there and then as a 14-year-old on running. Also, my decision to become a runner—well at this stage my decision to focus on running over soccer—goes back to what we were talking about earlier and my natural enjoyment of running. In soccer I was somewhat intimidated to make a tackle, or chase down the ball; I was afraid that I might get hurt. Whereas in running . . . wow, what a feeling. Shoes on . . . out the door, and boy I just went. There was no stopping me. I could tell that inside of me I had the freedom and the energy to go and go; I wasn't about to get hurt, either. And that feel-good factor, along with the confidence I got from athletics, was something I didn't experience doing anything else. I think as a runner I just always had a good idea of where I stood or what was possible.

Like predicting you'd run a 3:53 mile when your best time was only 4:01?

Exactly. Don't get me wrong, though, that wasn't arrogance. To begin with, I wrote that time down behind the mirror, didn't I? It wasn't like I was bragging to everyone, *I'm going to run 3:53 this year* . . . blah, blah, blah. It was just a mark that seemed appropriate to me. And with my newfound dedication, why not aim high?

Were there occasions during that year when you needed to turn the mirror around to remind yourself that this was going to be your sub-four year?

Once in a while, but again it's that confidence I had. I knew I was going to get under four that year. Even during the indoor season when I must have run four minutes flat three or four times, and the other guys at Villanova were beginning to ask me when was I finally going to break four, I remained confident. More importantly, Jumbo was confident. He said, "Just do the work, Coghlan, and the times will come to you." And I really believed that.

It seems like you always had a lot of faith in the men in your life—your father, Gerry, Jumbo?

I did. They were very important to me, all those men. Without them I'm not sure what I'd be doing today, or where I would've ended up. Because to be honest with you, besides sport I didn't have much going for me as a boy. For example, I'd come home from school and my parents would ask me if I had any homework and I'd say, "Ah, no." And then I'd go outside and play. My mother tried to interest me in the piano or Irish dance, but no way was I going to be seen doing that. Dancing was for sissies, I thought. Although, look at it now; maybe I could have been a superstar in *Riverdance*? But we had a little green area in the middle of our housing estate that we called the Field, and we used to play every sport there depending on the season. If it was Wimbledon we played tennis; if there was a big match at Lords we played cricket. We also played racing. And whenever it came to picking relay teams, I was always picked first. But more than that, I ran everywhere as a boy, including a mile and a half to school and back home for lunch and then back again. I ran to town for errands; I ran to my friends' houses; I ran to my girlfriend's. My routines and patterns were a bit like the Kenyans' today, I suppose. I became fit and strong partly by accident. And like I've been saying to you, I loved the feeling of my body moving fast, especially when it was effortless and easy, which, I have to admit, was how my first sub-four-minute mile felt when I finally did it, totally effortless, like a stroll through the park.

Can you tell me more about that?

Just like I had planned, I was a sophomore at Villanova and the Penn Relays were happening, and my father was coming over to see me run in America for the first time. So I thought, *Why not try to run my first sub-four-minute mile while my dad's in town?* Well, on a very warm, humid, and rainy Friday afternoon, I was the anchor man on our distance medley relay, which meant that I was to run a mile. And after the first three legs, I got the baton 30 yards behind a guy from Arizona State University. Immediately, I tore after him. Nothing else was on my mind except catching this guy. Finally, after working and working for three laps I caught him at the start of the final lap. But I had no idea how fast I had been running. That's a huge stadium at the University of Pennsylvania, and the crowd was going nuts. I couldn't hear Jumbo or anyone yelling splits. I couldn't even hear my father, although I knew he was out there somewhere.

Like I've been saying, it was winning the race that mattered to me. And when I got the stick 30 yards down there was only one thing to do: Set out for the leader. Anyway, after I caught him with a lap to go I sat behind him for the first turn. Then I decided to go myself. And right there, heading into the backstretch for the last time, bang, I put the hammer down and I was gone. Well, straight after I crossed the line one of the guys on the team came running up to me screaming and carrying on, "Eamonn, you did it, you did it." And I was like, "Yeah, I know, it's great, it's great we won the race." "No, no," he said, "you broke four minutes, you broke four minutes, you just ran 3:56." And I said, "What? You're joking." It was the easiest 3:56 imaginable. I remember absolutely nothing about the effort or the struggle or the pain or anything. Amazing, really, how something so significant and so important to me could just come out of the blue with hardly any effort at all.

Did some people question the legitimacy of your first sub-four-minute mile on a relay leg?

Yes, there would have been talk about that, and I would have agreed with it. But it was definitely under four minutes—and far enough too, that I knew any benefits of a relay leg couldn't have been that great. But anyway, two weeks later I had the opportunity to run a mile off start at the Pitt Invitational. And would you believe it, what do I end up running? Exactly what I ran on the relay leg, 3:56.2, to become "officially" a sub-four-minute miler.

So which race do you refer to as your first mile under four minutes, the anchor leg at the Penn Relays or the mile at the Pitt Invitational?

I refer to the Penn Relays because as far as I'm concerned I ran the mile distance under four minutes that day . . . although maybe I'd put an asterisk next it.

Did the sub-four-minute mile at Pitt come as easily for you as the one at the Penn Relays?

Nothing ever came as easily to me as that Penn Relays mile. But what I realized at Pitt was that I had a lot more in me. Heading down the home-stretch, I could tell that I wasn't using everything up, and Jumbo felt the same, which is why I was so anxious to keep racing, and why I went down to Jamaica the next week to run a mile against some of the best guys around, including Filbert Bayi from Tanzania who was the 1500-meter world-record holder. And I knew that this was going to be a fast race because Bayi was known for pushing the pace from the start. So my plan was to hang on for as long as I could. And sure enough, Bayi took off at the gun and I can tell you I was going for it all right. With half a lap to go I was in second place. Then finally I started to feel it in my legs, and down the homestretch Marty Liquori pulled beside me and I tried as best I could to hold him off but he just inched past me. And I don't know if you know this, but Bayi broke Jim Ryun's eight-year-old mile world record that night, running 3:51. And guess what my time was?

Was it . . ?

You got it, 3:53, exactly what I had written down on the back of my mir-ror nine months earlier. How's that for putting on a show?

Not bad, Eamonn. Not bad at all.

Photo: Colour Sport

# A Natural History

## SEBASTIAN COE
### (United Kingdom)

**First sub-4: August 30, 1976, 3:58.35, London**
**Personal best: 3:47.33**
**Total sub-4s: 11**

*W*herever there have been people, there have been stories. Human beings, after all, are storytelling creatures. Through language we make meaning out of experience and live within the stories we create. We gossip, we dream, we explain ourselves to others—all through story. Our own life stories are even fashioned into a beginning, middle, and end. In this way, says the Harvard psychologist, Jerome Bruner "There is no such thing as a 'life as lived' to be referred to. Rather, our lives are constructed and reconstructed by the act of autobiography."

The runner's story, however, is more often than not a story of records, times, and places. Language is subverted by numbers as the champion's tale revolves around the marks he set. And numbers don't lie. Two Olympic 1500-meter gold medals, for example. Or eight world records over the mile, 1500 meters, 1000 meters, and 800 meters. Is that the story of the greatest runner of all time? If so, it's a story that numbers alone can't do justice. Thank heaven, then, the author of that tale is willing to say some more.

Seb, as a former mile world-record holder, what advice would you give to an aspiring sub-four-minute miler?

I find it very frustrating when I speak to young milers today who don't know the history or evolution of their event. It was very important to me to be able to identify the key individuals who shaped the mile, and to know something about all the past Olympic 1500-meter champions. I was intrigued by their tactics, and inspired by their styles. I studied Herb Elliott, Peter Snell, Jim Ryun . . . well, the list of great milers goes on, doesn't it? And closer to my own time, I saw how Filbert Bayi and John Walker were rewriting the way 1500s and miles were run with their extreme emphasis on speed. Which was why when I entered university in 1976, I began to work out twice a week with the 400-meter squad. And for quite a few years, in fact, I was my university's anchorman on the 1600-meter relay. I could see that speed was going to increasingly become an essential ingredient in any distance event. History was making that quite clear. For example, Juha Vaatainen had won European titles at 5000 meters and 10,000 meters in 1971 with last laps approaching 50 seconds. And Emiel Puttemans had picked up medals at various distances by slinging in incredibly fast laps. And Miritus Yifter—or as he was known, "Yifter the Shifter"—was coming onto the scene, as well. One couldn't say any longer, *Oh, I'm a distance runner, therefore, I walk away from worrying about leg speed and speed drills.* You only had to look at the sport to see how it was changing. And at the same time, I think I saw the history of miling and distance running as my history: a tradition that I was hoping to enter one day. And so I considered it important to know what my place was in all of that. Which was why I read, and read, and read. And by 15 I had read almost every running biography published.

What were those biographies teaching you about running?

They were helping me understand what was required to become a world class miler. And for that reason, I found them very motivating. For example, the story of the 1954 Miracle Mile in Vancouver, when Roger Bannister and John Landy met for the first time as the world's only four-minute-milers, is a fascinating tale of rivalry, competition, and nationalism that would benefit any young runner today. Moreover, watching the tape of that race taught me a very important tactical lesson with regard to holding a lead, as Landy tried to do, and in many ways illustrated beautifully what not to do if you're in front coming down the final stretch—don't look left or right, but keep your eyes ahead.

What other tactical lessons did you learn from the greats?

Well, to understand how to take out a mile and hold a lead, study Herb Elliott's career. And to learn how to run from the back, watch Fermin Cacho's 1500-meter final at the Barcelona Olympics, in 1992, and notice how he picked up the pieces in the finishing straight. Now, to see how to throw a race away, watch my 800-meter final from the Moscow Olympics in 1980. There you'll see tactics gone totally wrong. But young runners should also study their contemporaries. When I watched my rivals run I'd think very carefully about what was unfolding, and how they were responding, and where they looked good in a race and where they looked bad. In a track race you make judgments all the time, and you should be constantly assessing your competitors' strengths and weaknesses.

Can you give an example of how something you learned about a particular runner helped you beat him?

Yes, going into the 1984 Olympic 1500-meter final in Los Angeles, I knew that Steve Cram was going to be a difficult competitor. But I knew something interesting about Steve, too. He was someone who gained confidence once he hit the front. His best mile and 1500-meter races all involved him winding up the pace with a lap or thereabouts remaining. My calculations before we met in Los Angeles told me that if he was leading going into the last lap he was likely to win. So I entered that Olympic final with one important tactic: *No matter what, I can't allow Steve to take the lead.* And I had settled in my own mind that even if that meant fighting him off with as many as two laps remaining, I was going to do it. I didn't care; I had to keep him behind me because I knew he didn't like chasing. And that's exactly what happened. Omar Khalifa took the pace out, followed by Steve Scott, and then Jose Abascal. At every lead change I was two or three strides back, with Steve another two or three places behind me. Then, along the backstretch of the last lap with about 240 meters remaining, Steve came up on my shoulder to try to pass me and move into second. But I was ready for him, and I reacted instantly by sprinting away and moving past Abascal to grab the lead. And thankfully I was able to hold on and win the race and survive what for me had been a very difficult year healthwise.

Speaking of the history and evolution of the mile, what kind of standard do you think a four-minute mile is today?

A very high standard. In saying that, however, one first has to distinguish between the physiological and the straightforward rankings list. It's true that a four-minute mile may not rank you very high in the world, but it is still an extremely difficult human endeavor. It is harder to run a sub-four-minute mile, in fact, than it is to run a 2:20 marathon. There are many, many more people who are capable of running under 2:20 for a marathon than are ever going to get under four minutes. It is a tough thing to do. It is running four consecutive laps at a pace which, according to current physiological assessments, is as demanding aerobically as it is anerobically. The athlete must buffer an extremely high level of lactic acid that begins to form about three-quarters of the way through, and of course still carry on at a very good clip. And if you think about it, there really haven't been that many people who have done it since 1954. Not even 1000, I suspect. And in half a century of development in a sport, that's not a lot. Especially when you consider the advances that have taken place in other sports over the same time period. For example, many top milers from the 1950s, someone like Derek Ibbotson springs to mind, would almost certainly qualify as an international today. Would that be the case with a top footballer or rugby player from that era? Could they play with today's best? Probably not. That's why we must never lose respect for the difficulty of a four-minute mile even though the current world record is quite a bit faster.

But you made running under four minutes, and a whole lot faster, actually, look anything but difficult.

Okay, but don't forget the showman effect. Believe me, there were many occasions during training when you would have seen me looking significantly more distressed than I ever did in a race. That was because the moment I walked into a stadium, or out of a changing room and onto the track, my whole demeanor would change. I used to believe that my races actually began the second I arrived at the village, or the hotel. And I would do my utmost to look confident and exude a strong presence. That is, the presence of someone who believes he will win. And I would study my competitors in the holding room of an important championship, too, in order to detect who was nervous or unsure. Competition, after all, brings out those vulnerabilities in people. It's why I admire boxing. The best boxers, you know, actually like a fight. They don't sit there before a fight thinking, *Oh, my God, I might go into that ring and end up on an oxygen tank.* Guys like Ali and Sugar Ray Leonard actually enjoyed the physical process of slugging it out toe to toe. It was something they regarded as a great challenge. And my feeling about racing was very similar. I relished the contest as an end in itself.

Were there instances during your career when you knew you were unfit, but by maintaining this "presence" you've referred to you were still able to intimidate your opponents?

I never thought it was very sensible to reveal one's vulnerabilities prior to a race. There were always those athletes who liked to get their excuses in early. They might say how they were recovering from an injury, or that they had lost some time training for one reason or another. I never did that. Why do something that can only help somebody else? Because if I knew that someone had just had three weeks off because of an injury, then I knew he must be a bit short on speed endurance. That, then, became something I could exploit by, for example, putting in the boot on the third lap and not allowing the pace to slacken.

Were there ever occasions when someone else's presence eliminated you from a race?

I would have to say, yes, once, in 1985 . . . Steve Cram. We met over the mile in Oslo on July 27, ten days after he had set a new 1500-meter world record in Nice. I wasn't in great shape, but Crammie was absolutely flying that night. After just two laps I knew I was working too hard and that this guy was running for fun from the front. On the backstretch of the last lap I knew that this was his day and that my world record was history. I still ran 3:49, which isn't bad, but Steve was literally unstoppable, and I had sensed that from the gun. On occasions like that there is really nothing you can do. John Walker said exactly the same thing about me in 1979 when I broke his mile world record. He said he knew within the first lap that his record was gone. And he told me afterward that he saw something in me that night, even before the race began, that indicated to him that I was on top of my game, and that no matter what he did he wasn't going to beat me.

Seb, this idea of "knowing" yourself and your competitors that you've just mentioned a few times, what is that exactly? Because it's not facts you're talking about, is it?

I think there is some degree of embodied running knowledge that every runner possesses. And that's not something that can be quantified, or isolated and examined in a precise or empirical manner. I suppose it's instinctual knowledge, and where it lies or how one taps into it is a mystery. But it's probably one of the most powerful and effective means a runner has to judge his own and others' capabilities. You instinctively know, for example, what kind of shape you're in based on what you've done in the past and what your responses have been to different types of workouts. So while the times you post in a training session are a useful indication of your fitness, I believe there is another realm of knowledge that can be used to determine how you're progressing, and that bit of information, that "feeling" you have about this or that, is sometimes the most important to possess.

Did you always possess an inner knowledge or feeling about your future as a runner?

That conclusion presented itself more directly, actually. There was a workout I did when I was about 13, and it was a cold and rainy night. If I recall, I was doing a session on a muddy field somewhere and my father, who was also my coach, was there timing me. As always he had my sweats wrapped around his neck so that as soon as I finished I could put them on. After I was done I was covered in mud and standing beside my father soaking wet with my track suit in my hands, when he began speaking in this very earnest tone. And he said, "Now, son, I don't want this to come as a surprise to you, but you will be an Olympian one day. So I think it's best if you start getting used to that idea sooner rather than later." You see, he knew even better than I did what he was seeing; he knew I was going to be a world beater even when I was just 13. And knowledge like that, whether in sport, business, or anything else, only comes from years and years of practice and trial and error.

What effect did your father telling you that have on you?

It was one of those moments that I will forever remember. Because without trying to sound arrogant, I knew he was right. And I knew it was time for me to begin thinking seriously about my future as an athlete.

Can I ask you what directed you into running first of all?

From a fairly young age I recognized that I wasn't ultimately suited to being the archetypal team player. While I appreciated the camaraderie of traveling with a good team, it would have absolutely infuriated me to have been totally committed to my sport only to be let down by a guy in another position who didn't have his life in order or his priorities straight. It must be dreadful to be gifted and talented as an individual football player, for example, but never have won anything because you were always on a poor team. I enjoyed the control over my own destiny that running afforded. And ultimately, I was prepared to accept both winning and losing. Obviously, you don't want to lose, you want to win, and you want to win more than you lose, but by and large if I was beaten by someone younger, fitter, and stronger, I accepted that. That was part of the process of competing in an individual sport: accepting responsibility for your outcomes. And generally that was a concept of sport that I was comfortable with.

Was there much support in your community to be a runner?

Unlike America at that time—that is, 1972 and post Frank Shorter and the running boom, where heading out the door for a run was almost admired as a positive, healthy thing to do—running in the UK back then practically qualified you as some kind of nut case. And when people in my hometown of Sheffield, which was an urban, northern industrial city, saw me putting in 3 or 4 miles before school, I think they wondered if I was mad, or if my father who was there urging me on should be reported to welfare services.

So what made you stick with it?

Because quite simply, I adored running. I still run today, in fact, and I find no better means of expression, or no better solace than through running. It's so exciting, it's a fantastic emotional outlet, and apart from spending time with my family there is nothing else that I can do for an hour that leaves me feeling more at one with myself and my surroundings. And running these days, I find, is particularly a luxury. Because when I was training for world records the running was so very hard. For example, I used to live in the most magnificent and scenic part of England, the Peak District in the north. And there would be 14- and 15-mile training runs I'd do that were absolutely stupendous. But they were also hard, and there were times when I'd be halfway through one of these runs and feeling exhausted but knowing that I had the same amount of distance to cover again. And I'd be thinking, *Stuff the surroundings, who cares about the expressive and aesthetic qualities of running, I just want this bloody run to end.* And track work was perhaps even harder than that. But now I run four or five days a week and my sole goal is to remain free from injury. I see running as a life time sport now, and I bless every day that I have the opportunity to go out running. Quite literally, running is vital in my day-to-day existence. There are times when I go out running with the idea of clarifying a problem, or sorting out some tasks. Other times running relieves any pressure I'm under. And when I return from a run I usually feel totally refreshed. Running is clearly mood altering, and a wonderful opportunity to focus on the physical and become one with yourself.

You mentioned the pain and hard work associated with your serious running life. Did you have any specific techniques to cope with that pain?

No.

What did you do then?

I don't know, I suppose I became immune to the pain. I didn't, for instance, try to focus on something else once the pain kicked in. I think I just learned to tolerate it instead. Partly, though, my training was so hard that any discomfort I had to put up with in a race was almost like having a day off. And when I went to a championship and ran heats and rounds over the course of a few days it was like having a week off. People often talk about my performance in the Los Angeles Olympics, when I ran both the 800 meters and the 1500 meters and competed in seven races over nine days, as being very tough. But I can assure you that it wasn't nearly as tough as some of the training sessions I ran back to back six months earlier.

While 1984, Seb, was possibly the pinnacle of your career, I'm interested in knowing whether at the beginning of your career, when you were first emerging on the British miling scene, you felt any added pressure to succeed as a miler because of the great tradition of British miling?

I don't think any British athlete with pretensions towards running middle distance can come through the ranks without recognizing that Great Britain was steeped in running lore and legacy. So yes, I was aware of the British tradition of miling; and yes, I was aware of Roger Bannister's achievements. But was it daunting to me? The answer is no. My more immediate frame of reference as a beginning runner was the standard expected of me by my local athletics club. But in reflecting on the mile's history and place in Britain, I think the situation here would be entirely different if Bannister hadn't run that first-ever four-minute mile. If Landy had done it instead, or maybe Wes Santee, I think the focus on miling would have turned away from Britain. And as a result, young British milers wouldn't have quite the same feeling for the four-minute mile as they do. In that sense, being British and running the mile is a connection that no British runner can ever shake.

Can you remember when four minutes as this suitably British standard first became something you respected and understood?

It was really never that big an issue in my head. I never sat around thinking, *Oh, I hope it's this weekend that I break four minutes.* I suppose I thought it was inevitable. After all, I had done what most people did. I ran 4:20, then 4:18, then 4:12, then 4:08, and when I started to regularly run 4:05 and 4:04, I thought, *Well, one big jump and it'll be done.*

Was there a particular moment when you knew that your first sub-four was around the corner?

Probably in early August 1976, when I went to a regional meet in Manchester and ran an 800. At that stage my best 800 time was 1:50.7, but I ended up running 1:47.4 that day. And I was quite stunned by that because it took me from oblivion to top five on the British ranking list. And I remember driving home with my father and him saying to me, "Well, that's very good news for your mile."

Was it then that you and your father planned your assault on four minutes?

To be perfectly honest with you, I don't think I ever discussed running under four minutes with my father. It was never an objective or a deliberate strategy of ours to try and get me under four minutes. I'm sorry to have to say that because I'm sure that's not what you want to hear for your book, but it really wasn't. I knew it would be a fantastic achievement when I did it, but that was about as far as I went in terms of thinking about four minutes as a premeditated goal.

Even after you ran 4:01.7 behind John Walker in Gateshead on August 21, a couple of weeks after the Manchester 800, you didn't think, *Oh, shoot, I just missed four minutes?*

I didn't, because times were always incidental for my father and I. He felt that if I raced properly, that was the definition of a good outing.

What do you mean by *racing properly?*

If I didn't hide, and I ran with style, determination, and commitment, my father was happy. That was why I once ran 1:43.9 for 800 meters in a small county championship, that was how I broke the mile world record in Oslo in 1979. I didn't have specific times on my mind in those races. I was simply trying to satisfy my father's criteria of good running, which meant displaying mental strength and style. Okay, if the time was good, as well, he'd acknowledge that, but times didn't fuel his ambitions as a coach.

What does *running with style* mean?

Showing good form most of all. For example, running tall and looking smart. But also being creative, or doing something different. And not being afraid to put others under pressure while at the same time demanding a lot from yourself.

Do you think you displayed style in your first sub-four-minute mile?

I do. Because I jumped to the front from the gun and led a world-class field for more than three laps. I remember thinking that day, *I have nothing to lose, and there's no point sitting back and waiting for something to happen.* I was coming off that 1:47 performance, you see, and I really didn't think that any sort of reasonable pace like 1:57 or 1:56 could tire me out. So my goal that day was to find out how long I could sustain a lead before the world caved in. After all, that was how I saw my style developing: putting myself so far ahead of a field that no one could catch me. In 1976, though, I was still learning how to do that, and it showed when seven guys passed me on the homestretch. But my feeling was that I would get better and better at that tactic. I just needed to practice it more. And all right, my world did cave in on the last lap, but I was very proud of how I ran.

Were you also proud that you broke four minutes?

Extremely so, especially because I didn't just sneak under four. I got a fair way under. I was also conscious that I had now joined a pretty elite running club, the sub-four-minute mile club, and being British, as I told you earlier, made that even more meaningful.

Did you have a special celebration after that race?

Not really. I had a very close-knit family, as well as close friends and training partners, so I was together with them that night. But you know, there was also an expectation among everyone around me that I would go on to run much faster than that 3:58. And because of that, I think, no one felt a particular need to celebrate wildly that night.

What do you think gave your friends and training partners such high expectations of you?

Remember, these were the people who watched me train every single day. And I'm sure they saw on my part a huge commitment to running, as well as some aptitude and desire. And as we know, those are vital ingredients for success.

What kind of status did breaking four minutes carry in British track back in 1976?

In 1976 Britain's position in the world of middle-distance running was quite weak. In a sense, very similar to what it is today. For instance, I didn't have any immediate role models of middle distance whom I wanted to emulate. You had to go back to the 1930s and 1950s for that. So when I broke four minutes it really meant something on the domestic front, unlike a few years later when Brits totally dominated the world mile scene and four minutes barely earned you a county title.

You said earlier that four minutes wasn't a barrier for you. What about breaking other benchmarks, like 3:50?

No, that wasn't a barrier either. I just didn't think about my career that way. For example, I never sat around thinking that I wanted to be the first man to run under 1:42 for 800 meters, which was something I did end up doing. I was never obsessed with times. I was much more steeped in the history of the sport and doing my best to make a lasting impression as a miler. I was also more interested in the nature of the people I was running against. I never judged other runners by their times, for example, but by their character and the way they ran. That was why a guy from America running 1:45

in May never worried me because I knew that he had probably benefited from great weather over the winter and that most likely he would be nowhere to be seen by July when the important races really began.

So if times were never barriers for you, were people?

I'm not sure *barrier* is the right word, but in terms of the mile, yes, there was one individual in my career who I looked at and thought, *You are very, very special.* And I knew I would have to get past him if I was going to win titles and set world records. I also knew that wasn't going to be easy. Of course, I'm talking here about Steve Ovett. And our rivalry was an interesting one because it wasn't like Jim Ryun sitting around wondering what Kip Keino was doing in the Nandi Hills, or John Walker thinking, *I wonder what Filbert Bayi is doing in Dar es Salaam.* I had this guy 180 miles down the motorway from me. He was ever present over my career. But that was a strength, as well. Because with the two of us and later Steve Cram, we were able to dominate the mile and 1500 meters for close to 10 years.

Would you call that period the greatest in British middle-distance running history?

That's for others to say, not me. But I hope future generations of British milers will study what we did because I think that's the only way they're going to be able to repeat it.

Photo by Colour Sport

# Iron Runner

## STEVE SCOTT
### (United States)

**First Sub-4: January 15, 1977, 3:59.7, Los Angeles**
**Personal best: 3:47.69**
**Total Sub-4s: 137**

*J*oe *DiMaggio carried a hitting streak through almost half a season. Lou Gehrig, and later Cal Ripken, played in consecutive games for more than 10 years. All three survive as iron men of baseball: resilient and consistent, not to mention world class. Who, then, is America's running iron man? Whose career spanned Olympiads? Who ran a record number of sub-four-minute miles? Only one man has the stuff of all that . . .*

*It's true that the runner's life is sometimes enviable—fine hotels and sumptuous meals around the world: Zurich, Berlin, Stockholm, and Paris. Not to mention the excitement of victory and the challenge of commitment. But there's a downside—losses, injuries, doubts. And the very ordinary regularity of the same yearly routine: training and racing, training and racing. This is what the sport philosopher, Dan Chambliss called "the mundanity of excellence." The sportsman's acute attachment to detail, his uncompromising nature, and his insistence on "getting everything just right." As a result we have the miler as perfectionist: the consummate "hard-at-work" professional*

*whose reward is a spectacular run at the top; whose reward is a legacy that survives a*
*generation on.*

Steve, of all the cool and exciting things you could have been doing as a
California kid back in the 1970s, why running?

You know, that's a perception people in other parts of America have about
Californians, that we like to cruise along and take things really easy. But
California kids, and track kids in particular, aren't necessarily like that; they
aren't afraid to push themselves and set goals. In some senses kids here work
harder than kids from other parts of the country because the weather is
always so good. Although I suppose I should admit I wasn't like that. In fact,
as a kid I would look for any excuse possible not to go running.

Didn't you like to run?

Oh sure, I was just real lazy when it came to training. The only workouts
I did in high school were the ones my coach supervised. And in front of him
I'd bust a gut. Other than that, though, like on Sundays or over the summer,
when I was supposed to run on my own, forget about it. I'd only go out for
a run if one of my teammates came around to my house and got me.

What did you like to do instead of putting in your run?

I don't know, just mess around. It wasn't that I deliberately avoided running because I had better things to do. I just had absolutely no work ethic
whatsoever. On a Sunday, for instance, I'd keep putting my run off, and putting it off. And then I might get hungry, so I'd go and have something to eat;
then something else would usually come up and I'd get involved in that, and
before I knew it it'd be dark and I'd be like, Oh well, there goes that day's
training.

Would you feel guilty when that happened?

Not really. In high school I wasn't really thinking long term about my
running. I was just doing my own thing and having fun. I suppose I wasn't

mature enough at that point to believe I was hurting my chances to succeed by not training my hardest.

Why run the mile, then—an event that demands a lot of work and dedication?

The mile does demand a lot of work, you're right about that. Which was why I tried to have as little to do with it as possible. It was just too hard. I mainly ran the 800 in high school. I think my best mile time was only about 4:15, and that came on a relay.

So what was it that eventually led you to become a miler?

Well, it wasn't my idea, I can assure you that. It was all the doings of my college coach, Len Miller. You see, I ran cross-country in high school so I did have a decent amount of strength, but primarily I thought of myself as a fast guy, not a distance runner. I could run a decent 400, for example, and Dave Wottle, the 800 Olympic champion in 1972, was one runner I admired. I loved the way he came from behind on the last lap with a big, strong kick. That was my racing strategy as well: to kick hard over the final 100. So in my mind, my future was all the 800. Besides, I really liked running 800s. Probably because it was such an easy event for me due to the strength I had built up running cross-country. Maybe I'd get a little tired over the last bit, but that was all. I never got that deep-down tired like I did when I ran the mile. But when Len was recruiting me he had definite plans to turn me into a miler. One night, even, he came to my house and sat down next to me and my mom on the living room sofa and said in this dead-serious, matter-of-fact way, "Steve, if you come to the University of California at Irvine, I'm going to make you into the next American record-holder in the mile."

What did you say to that?

Well, to be honest with you, I was totally against the idea. For starters, I didn't like the mile, and apart from Wottle I didn't know about any other big-name runners. I didn't know who ran the mile, or even what the American record was. I wasn't the type of kid to sit at home and study *Track and Field News.* So when Len said that to me, about becoming the next American-record holder in the mile, it didn't register at all. Thinking about it now, I don't think I understood what he meant. I mean, I had never thought of myself in those terms before, as a miler. And I certainly wasn't flattered if that was his intention. To become the American-record holder in the mile was almost laughable to me then. So, really, because it came totally out of left field, I basically blew it off.

What do you think Len saw in you to make such a statement?

I suppose he saw my strength to handle cross-country, plus my 400 speed. Also, as a kid I was big and strong. So maybe he thought I'd be able to handle that degree of work. But I wasn't going to have anything to do with his plans. And that was what I told him, too. I told him I wanted to be an 800-meter runner, not a miler.

And what did he say?

He played it cool. He said what any smart recruiter would: "All right, Steve, we'll see." Which was definitely the right thing for him to say. Because in order for me to commit to the mile, I had to see it and believe it myself. It wasn't something I could do for Len. And Len knew that, which was why he was so patient with me.

What finally brought you around to his way of thinking?

Well, from my very first day on the Irvine campus, Len began telling me stories about the mile: what a good time was, who guys like Roger Bannister, Jim Ryun, and Peter Snell were, and who held the American record and the world record. And he told me about Filbert Bayi and John Walker and some of their classic duels. And then Walker became someone I started to admire. He had a similar body type to me, and I thought his long hair and beads were cool. He was also into partying and drinking and womanizing, whereas most of the top distance runners in the U.S. at that time, guys like Frank Shorter and Dave Wottle, were pretty square and kind of nerdish. Then I began to have some success following Len's training program, first in cross-country and then later in track. And then in my sophomore year, which was 1976, I had a huge breakthrough at the Olympic trials. I ran 3:40 for 1500 meters in my semifinal and advanced to the finals. And I realized then that Len must know what he's talking about. Because for me to reach the finals of the Olympic trials after only two years of training like a miler must mean something. So I said to myself, *Okay, that's it, I'm a miler now.*

Really, your transformation into a miler occurred that suddenly?

Oh, absolutely. Everything really came together for me at the trials that year; it was a complete turning-point experience. And at once, as if someone had flicked on a switch, I could see that Len was right, and that my talent did lie in the mile, not the 800. Another thing that had a big effect on me that week was on the morning following the 1500-meter finals when I went down to have breakfast. There standing in front of me was a group of guys who had just come in from a fifteen-mile run. Let me tell you, that was an eye-opening experience. I remember thinking, *Here I am just stumbling out of bed and these guys have already been out running for close to two hours.* For the first time in my life I actually felt guilty for being so lazy and uncommitted. And essentially, from that day onward no one ever had to remind me or pester me to do a workout. More than anything else, I wanted to train.

What exactly was it about making the finals of the Olympic trials that motivated you? Was it fulfilling some new vision you had of yourself as an Olympian or a world-record holder?

It dawned on me how much harder than me these other American milers worked, yet I still made the Olympic trials finals. So I asked myself, How good could I be if I ran every day and did all the other little things that I knew I needed to do? Also, the idea of being an Olympian really hit me, too. When I realized how close I actually came to making the Olympic team, I was like, *Wow, that's so cool.* So I think having a little taste of that level of success, and really liking it, too, made me want to have more. I think in one way it became like a drug to me: to succeed and win races, to gain the admiration of other people, and to try to become an Olympian. To be quite honest with you, my whole reaction to events at the trials really surprised me. I had no idea that deep down inside of me there was this powerful will and drive to be the best. That meet certainly unearthed it, though. And beginning almost immediately, I started to get up early to run, and I began to lift weights, eat right, and go to bed before ten o'clock. I started to do all the stuff I knew I should have been doing all along, but that I just couldn't motivate myself to do.

Did your Olympic trials breakthrough also make you think, *Now I can become a sub-four-minute miler?*

Oh, yeah. Four minutes was always a big goal for me. And you're right, after the trials I knew it was going to happen. I knew, after all, that 3:40 for 1500 meters was quite a bit better than 3:59 for a mile.

When did you expect to run your first four-minute mile?

Right away, really. In other words, the next outdoor season when track started again. So the fact that I ended up doing it that winter instead came as a real surprise. I wasn't even thinking about racing that indoor season at all, but when the opportunity came up to run the Sunkist Meet in Los Angeles against some top guys like Paul Cummings and Wilson Waigwa, Len thought it might be a good idea for me to experience running indoors in a big invitational. But I hadn't done any specific training to prepare myself for a four-minute mile. I even turned up at the starting line wearing cross-country flats because I didn't own a pair of spikes suitable for a wooden track. And my only race plan was to stay as close to the leaders as I could, and if I had anything left at the end, then great, I'd go for it and see what happened. And that was exactly how the race went. I got sucked along without really doing anything or knowing too much at all, and bang, suddenly I was a sub-four-minute miler.

Was there a point during that race where you thought, *Hey, this is going better than I expected, maybe I can break four minutes?*

No. Honestly, breaking four minutes that night never entered my mind once.

But you must have thought it was within the realm of possibilities. After all, you had just run the equivalent of a 3:57 mile a few months earlier.

You know why I wasn't considering it? Because I had always had this image in my mind of a sub-four-minute mile as this exhausting effort that required one's complete attention and focus. So while I was confident that I would eventually break four minutes one day, I thought it would require this extended period of specific preparation and hard work, followed by a detailed race plan. Whereas in Los Angeles that night, all I was trying to do was stay close to the leaders. Really, I was just out there competing as best I could without thinking about too much else. That was it. For example, I never heard any splits, or anyone screaming out to me that I was on four minute pace. But right after I crossed the line someone did say to me, "Hey, Scott, you just broke four minutes." And I'll tell you, I was real surprised. I was surprised, mainly, by how easy it felt. Because in reality it didn't feel too different from any other race, when I was expecting it to be this momentous event.

Did that race change the way you thought about yourself as a runner like your Olympic trials performance did?

More than my 3:40 at the Olympic trials, that race kind of put me in the spotlight. To be only a college junior running a sub-four-minute mile was a big deal back then. So I had to do a few interviews and other stuff with the media. To most people looking in from the outside at me and my running, that 3:59 appeared to be this miraculous breakthrough that came out of the blue. But for me it felt like a natural progression; I expected it, and I was prepared for it. After all, I had been steadily improving each year. So overall the effect on me wasn't that great or startling. But my next mile race, a month later in San Diego, that was a different story. My result there had a big impact on me because of who I beat. You see, in Los Angeles I had the time breakthrough and got under four minutes for the first time—which was fantastic, but I didn't really beat anyone. In San Diego, though, I was lining up next to my hero John Walker, and other guys like Eamonn Coghlan. So when I finished second behind Wilson Waigwa and actually beat Walker and Coghlan, and also improved my time to 3:56, that, I'll tell you, was an incredible feeling and just absolutely huge for me. I could hardly believe it at first: to beat John Walker, the Olympic champion and mile world-record holder. So really, more than any other race that one in San Diego set the stage for my future in track. Because that was when it dawned on me that not only could I possibly become the top miler in America, but maybe I could become one of the top milers in the world.

And what a future it was, Steve. In fact, you really belonged to an incredible era of talent and depth in the mile. Was that something you were aware of while it was happening?

Oh, yeah. Because I'd look back at results when Peter Snell was the top miler around, and then later Jim Ryun, and I noticed how they were always way out in front in their races and consistently winning by three or four seconds. But for me and the other guys from my era, like Walker, Coghlan, Steve Ovett, Ray Flynn, Seb Coe, Steve Cram, Said Aouita, Thomas Wessinghage . . . I mean the list just goes on and on, that was never the case. The mile world record was being broken quite regularly, and by someone different every time, and every race was close with the results for second and third sometimes good enough to end up on the top five all-time list. It was just crazy how competitive the circuit was back then. I remember one year, I think it was 1981, when there was something like 10 guys who had run under 3:50. I think it's safe to say that we've never seen that kind of depth since. And while it was a real thrill to be part of that period, sometimes I think, *Dang, I could have probably been number one in the world any other year.* But, you know what, I don't think any of us would have run as fast as we did if it wasn't for the fact that we were constantly being stretched to think differently about how fast a man could run a mile. And this wasn't only happening outdoors—superfast races week after week, new world records—it was happening indoors, too.

Speaking of indoors, was the rhythm of running a mile indoors different for you than running a mile outdoors?

I must say I never felt comfortable running indoors on the boards. Outdoors I had more room to move, and I could settle into my stride and generate a nice even, consistent cadence. My legs were just too long for indoor tracks, so during a race I'd constantly have to shorten my stride, then lengthen it, and that never felt right to me. The key to my running well was having a smooth and economical stride. I just loved the feeling of continual, uninterrupted movement, and a controlled steady pace. That way I could keep out of trouble and avoid getting boxed in; and I could hold my rhythm and concentrate on finishing strong. Whereas if guys were messing around with silly tactics, or I got thrown off stride or tripped up, it was really hard for me to recover. Even worse were races that went out really fast, like in 53 seconds for the first lap. They gave me so much trouble because immediately I was taken out of my comfort zone. In order for me to run well I needed to feel that internal sense of being on the right pace. So if I felt I was running a step too fast, or a step too slow, or maybe my breathing was heavier than normal, that usually meant I was in for a bad race.

Was running a bad race something that worried you?

Not really, because I always knew that waiting for me around the corner was an opportunity to redeem myself. I never dwelled on my defeats, because quite frankly, I didn't have time. I was always getting ready for my next race.

Do you think you ran too many races over your career?

I do. I can see that now. And I definitely ran tired in a lot of my races. But I was following John Walker's lead. He was always out there racing, so I figured I might as well, too. You also have to realize that back then no one was paying our living costs in Europe. So after we ran a race and got kicked out of the hotel, we needed to find someplace else to stay. That usually meant running another race and moving into the next hotel on the circuit. On top of that, there was also a greed factor. Over in Europe, I was getting paid to race, not to sit around and train or rest, so my thinking was, *Why not make it while I can?*

Was all the racing you did connected in any way to accumulating a record number of sub-four-minute miles?

That wasn't even something I was aware of until John [Walker] and I started approaching 100. I don't know who it was, but some journalist noticed when we were around 70, and after that reporters began asking us who was going to reach 100 first. It ended up being John mainly because he had the advantage of running outdoors in New Zealand through December and January.

But you ended up with the most.

That's right, I did. And that's not counting all the 1500s I ran below 3:42, which is roughly the equivalent of a sub-four-minute mile. So God knows how many I would have done if those counted, too.

Was your first sub-3:50 mile in any way as significant to you as your first sub-four?

No, I'd say the first sub-four meant more. My first race under 3:50 [3:49.68, Oslo, 1981] was kind of disappointing actually. At that stage in my career my sights were set almost exclusively on breaking the mile world record. So I wasn't thinking in terms of just trying to get under 3:50. I wanted that world record. And I missed it that night in Oslo by less than a second. Even the fact that I smashed Jim Ryun's American record by one and a half seconds didn't make me feel any better. My attitude, was, *Well, that's all well and good to break the American record, but I've got bigger goals in mind.*

Do you think your American record [3:47.69, Oslo, 1982] is under threat anytime soon?

Not as far as I can see. We haven't really had a truly world-class American miler in quite some time. But you never know who might emerge in the near future.

Is the mile in jeopardy of becoming an obsolete event in America?

Absolutely not. But it is true that American sports fans only care about seeing Americans do well. So right now when we don't have an American miler among the world's top five, the mile's not going to receive much attention. But you know, that can change overnight. Just look at all the hype that followed Alan Webb a couple of years ago when he broke Jim Ryun's high school record. So I think the mile's in good health in this country. In fact, I think Americans are salivating for someone to come along and mix it up with El Guerrouj and Lagat, and some of the other top guys. Certainly, that was always my aim: to be the best miler in the world, and bring the record back to America.

# A New Breed of Miler

## STEVE CRAM
### (United Kingdom)

**First sub-4: July 2, 1978, 3:57.42, London**
**Personal Best: 3:46.32**
**Total sub-4s: 34**

*L*ondon and all its tradition and history: Westminster, Trafalgar Square, the monar-chy, Tower Bridge, the River Thames. London's also the home of modern track and field's rules and records, set down in 1834. Also in London the first intercollegiate athletics meeting took place (Cambridge versus Oxford, 1860), and the first interna-tional (Oxford versus Yale, 1894)—thus beginning decades of British middle-dis-tance running dominance, over the mile especially.

Tall, wide-shouldered, and strong, Steve Cram was one English miler who always assumed the lead. Slow pace, fast pace, or sustained charge—he knew how to deliver the necessary tactics. A child prodigy who first broke four minutes at 17, he sits before me now in the lounge of the St. James Court Hotel, a stone's throw away from Buckingham Palace. Still trim and blond, he seems a content ex-mile world record-holder.

Throughout the 1980s Cram was posting top times and consistent results: three

*Olympic 1500-meter finals (1980, 1984, 1988), and three world records over 19 days in 1985, including the mile on July 27. He belonged to the first generation of milers—Coe, Ovett, Aouita, Scott, Abascal—who earned a healthy living racing around the globe. He contributed to the changing face and the changing fortune of running— appearance fees, bonuses, television rights, endorsements. The standards and procedures in track and field were being rewritten, and much of it happened here in London. To understand the mile and its shifting social history, therefore, we need to return to England; we need to talk to an '80s English miler.*

Steve, given such an illustrious tradition of British milers before you—and not just Coe and Ovett, but Wooderson, Bannister, and Ibbotson, all of whom held the world record—did you ever feel pressured to live up to the expectations of being a "British miler"?

Obviously there was no Coe and Ovett when I first got interested in athletics, which would have been in the late 1960s, when I was eight or nine years old. At that time we actually didn't have a big star in the mile. But certainly, yes, I was well aware that Britain should be doing well in that event. I knew who Roger Bannister was, for example, and the significance of his achievements, as well as Gordon Pirie, Derek Ibbotson, Chris Chataway, and what they had done. My dad was crazy about sport, and my uncle was a professional footballer, so the names of past British champions in all sports often came up in conversation in our house. But with respect to athletics, the names and stories I grew up hearing all had to do with the mile. I don't think I could have even named a famous British sprinter. In fact, there just weren't any. So slowly I began to associate being British with being good at the mile. But then in the early 1970s Dave Bedford appeared on the scene and began to do his stuff, and not long after that Brendan Foster, so my interest in distance running just grew and grew and grew very quickly. Dave and Brendan weren't milers, though, and I can remember the British press moaning about Britain's demise in the mile. And this, I think, had a particular effect on me and pushed me toward the mile as opposed to the longer races. In fact, in my first race ever in 1973, I ran a mile. That was around a five-lap track and I can't even remember my time. But anyway, when I was a kid there was really ly no question about what events you ran if you were interested in running: You ran anything from the mile up, including cross-country in the winter.

That was it. But with this came the feeling that you were participating in something that mattered, not only to yourself, your family, and your community, but the entire nation. And I can remember how that felt special . . . or satisfying.

But did that expectation of success ever feel like a burden to you?

Not at all. If anything it gave me more confidence. I believed that I was in the right sport, not some minority sport. And I believed that I was running the right event: the mile. I imagine it's a bit like how American sprinters must feel at the Olympics. Does the tradition of Jesse Owens and Carl Lewis make them nervous? I wouldn't think so. It's more of a reassurance that you're doing what you're supposed to be doing. And more importantly, that you are who you are supposed to be.

It's how identities form, isn't it, through traditions, cultural histories, and stories around the dinner table?

Exactly.

How do you think British milers today feel about themselves given all the success the African nations are experiencing in the distance events?

I don't think they have any confidence in themselves whatsoever. And that's understandable. They don't necessarily believe, like I did, that when a Brit chooses to be a distance runner he'll be successful internationally. And that's having a big effect because we do have talented guys out there; they just don't associate distance running with Britain anymore. For them those are African events now, so they have this inferiority complex; they've lost the psychological edge of tradition that we had in my day.

Speaking of dominant British sporting traditions, apparently you were quite a useful football player as a boy. How did you decide to pursue running over football?

Whew, that was hard. It was a very tough decision. But at 14, toward the end of the football season, which is about the start of the track season, I finished third in the All-England Schools Cross-Country Championships, which was a pretty high level. That spring I was playing football on Saturday mornings and running track in the afternoons. Finally my athletics coach told me that I had to decide which sport to do. And it was hard, very hard, but in the end I had to face the fact that as much as I loved football I was never going to be all that great at it.

And you believed, at just 14, that you could be a great runner?

I did. Although I never thought I'd go on to do what I did. But I'd already experienced some success at the national level, like my third place in the cross-country, whereas honestly I was just a good football player in my school, and not much beyond that. So I put all my eggs in one basket, so to speak, because more than anything I just wanted to be good at something, especially sport.

Once you committed yourself to running, who did you turn to for support?

Both my dad and my coach were fantastic. Even to this day my coach is a major influence in my life. He helped form my talent more than anyone, or at least he brought it out of me. And my dad was so very, very encouraging. He was a police officer and worked shifts. So what he would do was try to organize his schedule so he was free to bring me to my races. My parents along with my coach and his wife became best of friends and socialized a lot together, too. So in a way, they became this unit that looked after me and watched over my progress, especially in the early years. As I matured, though, Brendan Foster became more and more of an influence. That was something my coach encouraged because he thought I needed support and advice from someone who had competed at an international level, and seeing as Brendan was from the same area as me and living in the same town, he became the obvious choice to take on that role.

And what did Brendan do for you?

He knew so much about tactics and handling the pressure of big races, and he shared all of that with me. More importantly, he became a target for me to focus on. Because even though Brendan was my mentor, and I was only a teenager, I desperately wanted to beat him. It's all thanks to Brendan, in fact, that I ran my first sub-four-minute mile when I did. He was ahead of me with a lap to go, you see, and I was chasing after him, giving it my all to beat him. I actually passed him with 300 yards left, but he passed me back on the homestretch and outleaned me for third.

So you weren't afraid to go up against senior runners like Brendan?

Definitely not. I have to say that I was never afraid of racing people. My coach taught me that. Throughout my career we always focused on people, not times. We never began a season thinking about running such and such a time by the end of the year. It was always about beating certain people and winning. For example, when I was 14 I placed fourth in the English Schools 1500. The kid who beat me was from Leicestershire and so that summer my coach and I would go to races out there in order to settle the score with this kid.

Sounds like some Wild West shootout?

It was a bit, because we could have easily stayed at home and run in local meetings. But no, we hit the road in pursuit of this kid.

Did you avenge your loss to him?

No, but I did begin to close the gap. The point, though, is that I always had this idea that the way to move forward as a runner was to knock off the people ahead of you. My coach and I were always picking someone to beat; even on the Grand Prix circuit when I was running the big events in Zurich and Oslo, I'd have as my goal beating guys I had never beaten before. Mind you, not Coe or Ovett initially, but maybe John Walker, or Steve Scott, or somebody else that I hadn't already beaten. For me it was the only way to survive those races. Otherwise I could find myself stuck in no-man's-land between two groups of guys. It's a lot easier to run a race, I think, than chase a time.

So competition was the name of the game for you?

Absolutely. I can remember racing Brendan in a cross-country meet when I was only 16. I had no business at all being up with him, but I hung on his shoulder for 3 or 4 miles before he finally dropped me. My philosophy was that it was always better to find out where you stood and face losing than to go around with false expectations of yourself and your ability. Losing was never some personal defeat for me. It was a lesson, or feedback, if you will, about what I needed to work on. Maybe my speed was off, or my tactics were wrong? I could always learn from my races about how to improve.

Did the older, more established guys in British athletics accept you, this kid hanging off their shoulder and following them around?

Oh, they were fantastic. And I was conscious of that, not bothering guys with too many questions or turning into Brendan's lapdog. Everyone around me was supportive and helpful. Well, except for the officials at British Athletics. Bloody blazer brigade, they were, all high and mighty and trying to control the sport and everyone in it.

What do you mean?

British Athletics was the organization that ran our sport. They were based in London and so hardly knew that anyone else in the country existed. At 16 I set a UK age record for 1500 meters [3:47.07] but didn't even get named to any age-groups team, or training camps, or anything. It was because I was from the north, not London, I'm sure of it. But this went on into the next year as well and it became really frustrating. In fact, because my mother is German I considered running for Germany at one point.

You're kidding?

No. I had serious discussions with German officials about running for them.

So what happened?

Well, eventually I did begin to get some recognition at home and that placated my concerns, if you will. I became more involved in different national networks and regional training squads. At the same time athletics was becoming more businesslike with independent meet promoters and agents entering the scene. The first guy to really make an impression in this way was a chap named Andy Norman, who was naturally good mates with Brendan seeing as Brendan was the star of British athletics at this time. So by association Andy began to look after me, and that was when everything started to fall into place.

So was it Andy who gave you your entree into professional running?

Oh, my dear, that's a convoluted story. But I'll tell you because it relates back to that mile I ran against Brendan where I almost beat him and subsequently ran my first sub-four-minute mile, which is what I know you want to discuss given the focus of your book.

Great. Let's hear the story.

Okay, how I first came to get help from Andy was due to the fact that in my last year of high school, when I was 17, so this would have been 1978, I had been led to believe by officials at British Athletics that in June I'd be going to a training camp for a week with a squad of other British junior runners to prepare for the European junior championships later in the summer. Now offhandedly, I mentioned this to my schoolteacher—that I was probably going to be away for a week in June at a camp. As it turned out, though, scheduled for that same week were the trials to qualify from my region to run in the English schools championships, where I was the defending champion in the 1500. And thinking he was doing the right thing, my teacher didn't enter me because he thought I was going to be away. Fair enough, right? But as it turned out, as so many things did back then with British Athletics, I ended up not getting picked to go on this training camp. So back at school I told my teacher this, which was when he told me that he hadn't entered me in the trials for the English Schools. Big problem, right? Well, he immedi-

ately calls the Durham County athletics people to get me entered in the trials. But what do they say? No, entries had closed. So he keeps after them trying to explain the mix-up and convince them to reconsider but they won't
budge. Typical British beaurocrats: following procedures to the end and never
making any exceptions. Well, I can tell you that by this time I was bloody
well pissed off. First of all, it was a misunderstanding that my entry form had-
n't been submitted. It wasn't like we were doing something devious. Also,
my little county, Durham, had only ever had a few English Schools champions in its entire history and here I was a defending champion and they would-
n't let me run. Bloody ridiculous. Finally, though, they said I could run, but
only as long as no other schools protested my presence in the meet, which if
they did I would have to be disqualified. Well, that didn't appease me very
much. I was so annoyed by this attitude, and how stupid it would be to disqualify a kid who had every legitimate right to run. But because of this threat
to disqualify me, I decided that I was going to run so fast that day that anyone would be totally embarrassed to even think about disqualifying me. So
standing on the line waiting for the starter to call us to our marks—and I
hadn't discussed my plan with anyone else—I was thinking just one thing:
*blast off.* And when the gun went, I was gone: wire-to-wire, head down, in the
lead by miles, never looking back, and I ran 3:42.07, a five-second improvement on my personal best and nearly the equivalent of a four-minute mile.
Now, Brendan was in the stands watching all of this and he was like, *Holy
shit.* Straightaway he rang Andy to tell him that he had to invite me down to
the Emsley Carr Mile in two weeks' time at Crystal Palace. Now, this was one
of the most prestigious mile races in the country if not the world, but sure
enough, Andy invited me, and it was in that race where I almost beat
Brendan and ran 3:57.42, my first four-minute mile. But that's not even the
whole story. That summer the Commonwealth Games were on, and because
England, Scotland, and Wales competed as individual nations—unlike the
Olympics where everyone is under the Union Jack—it was English Athletics
not British Athletics who picked the English team. And Andy, you see, was
high up in English Athletics, so while I was warming down after my race, he
came up to me and asked me if I'd like to go to the Commonwealth Games.
And I was like, *Oh my God . . .* Oh, and that's right, my 3:57.42 was also a
world record for 17-year-olds.

Amazing story. So in two weeks you went from competing at your local county championships, to running your first sub-four-minute mile and setting an age-group world record, to getting selected for the Commonwealth Games.

That's right, and all because of stubborn athletics officials, ridiculous politics, and incompetence. Don't forget that. Because to begin with, I should have been at that camp and missed the county meet, but that was a screwup by British Athletics. Second of all, I never would have gone out and run that hard at the county meet if I hadn't been so angry about the Durham athletics officials threatening to disqualify me. And then I wouldn't have been invited to the Emsley Carr Mile . . . or set the record . . . or been picked for the Commonwealth Games . . . and on and on. So there you have it, the story behind my first four-minute mile and the launch of my international career all in one.

Great stuff, and, like you said, entirely fueled by anger and proving yourself.

Yeah, for some reason I've always been motivated to prove people wrong, especially anyone who doubted my ability. I'm not sure where that came from. To be honest, though, nothing could have prepared me for those two weeks between the county championships and the Emsley Carr Mile. It was all so unexpected, and such a whirlwind of events. I was completely overwhelmed.

How so?

It was headline news the following day. The back page of the *Daily Mirror* read, SCHOOLBOY BREAKS FOUR MINUTES. The attention was a lot to handle, and I was embarrassed about what to say to the press or how to react at school around my mates. My whole concept about myself as an athlete changed after that first sub-four. I started thinking, for example, that running is obviously something I'm very good at and that I'll probably be doing for a very long time. The next week at the English Schools Championships I had a very strange experience. First of all, everyone knew who I was on account of all the sub-four hype. Also, because I was such a hot favorite in the 1500 I felt like I had to win. Then the race started and people began to cheer for all the other guys. So on the one hand everyone was happy for me that I was a sub-four-minute-miler, and that I was named to the Commonwealth Games team, but on the other hand they wanted to see me lose. Very strange indeed. Anyway, I won the race. But I had to work for it. It wasn't a walkover by any means.

To some extent, Steve, you must have seen this coming. After your 3:47 for 1500 meters when you were 16, you had to have had an inkling that your first four-minute mile wasn't too far away?

Honestly, I didn't. Not a lot of guys were breaking four minutes in England then. Also, following that 3:47, which I ran in early May, I didn't improve the rest of the season. I was thinking that I could break four minutes at 18 or 19, but not 17. It wasn't until the 3:42 in my county meet that I accelerated my plans, especially because that race gave me the chance to run in a very high-quality mile field.

So you were thinking about breaking four minutes going into the Emsley Carr race?

Again, not really. Maybe only in the back of my mind. There were other things I was thinking about instead. First, the race was on television and I had never run on television before. I had never run in the Crystal Palace before, either, and to me that was the Mecca of running. Going down to London was a huge deal, too, and I really didn't know how to act or what to do at the meet. Like the morning of the race I went to breakfast in the hotel and I didn't know anyone so I just sat by myself. I was nervous about so many little things, like where to warm up, stuff like that. It wasn't that I was over-awed; everything was just new and strange, so much bigger, you know? But honestly, I just didn't want to embarrass myself on TV. Nothing else was an issue for me, like four minutes or the Commonwealth Games, except that. Eventually, I figured that the best way not to make a fool of myself was to follow Brendan, because he surely wasn't going to run a bad race. And so that's what I did, like I told you, until I went past him with 300 yards to go.

Did you have any idea of the pace and how fast you were running?

I hadn't heard any splits. I was simply racing, and working hard to keep up. Then, because of Brendan passing me at the line, I was too disappointed to think about my time or wonder if I had broken four minutes. It wasn't until a few minutes later when an official told me that I was well under four minutes that it dawned on me that I might have run a fast time, or at least a new personal best.

And what was your reaction when you finally did hear your time?

At first I was pretty cool about it. Like I said, I was a bit upset about Brendan outleaning me. But on the other hand, I knew that fourth in such a prestigious race was good, and then breaking four minutes was a big step. So I had mixed emotions initially. It wasn't until an hour or so when I learned I had run a world record for 17-year-olds . . . and then the Commonwealth thing with Andy . . . that I started thinking, *Bloody hell . . .*

 Did you think you were pretty hot stuff?

Well, that's the interesting thing about it, I really didn't. Second place in that race was Graham Williamson from Scotland . . . a teenager. And behind me in fifth was Tim Hutchings . . . a teenager. Also, Coe and Ovett were emerging then not just as good British milers, but as the world's best milers, and they really weren't that much older than me . . . 20, 21. So my ego was quickly kept in check.

At the same time it must have been inspiring to be surrounded by so many great milers. It's what we were talking about earlier, isn't it, how tradition and expectation breed confidence?

Oh, undoubtedly. My perspective on the mile then was that good teenagers broke four minutes. I didn't see that as anything extraordinary or unusual. And Seb and Steve were like a vanguard leading us all into another era of racing, promotion, and television. They did as much for middle-distance running as anyone before them. They took it into the 20th century, really. The way they ran so hard, and pushed the pace, they made the mile more like a sprint. That changed forever how athletes approached the mile.

So in this metric age, Steve, why do you think the mile still matters?

I think the tradition of four laps in four minutes appeals to every middle-distance runner regardless of where he is from. Also, promoters now have two events, the 1500 and the mile, for athletes to break records. And just look at the names on the mile world-record list. It's all the biggest names in the history of the sport; every runner wants to be part of that, even the Africans who didn't grow up with yards, feet, and inches. The mile was the blue ribbon event in track and field for so many years. Everyone knew about it. And then, of course, there was all this mystery with four minutes and why it took so long. That sort of stature doesn't disappear overnight. Frankly, I don't think it ever will.

What did you find interesting or challenging about the mile?

I liked how it combined so many different aspects of running like speed, strength, and tactics. Finding the right way to win a race also intrigued me. You had this short amount of time, roughly three and a half minutes, and you could just about afford to make one mistake, but that was all. Then you had to quickly put it right. I loved standing on the line before the gun sizing everyone up, trying to guess what different guys were thinking. This was before rabbits were dominant, so you had to be a strategist, and that appealed to me very much. In a mile there are no dead periods. It's all action, action, action.

From your vantage point now, what are the strongest memories you have of your career as a miler?

It's odd, but so many of my memories of races are actually the television pictures rather than my own memories. And it's those images that get reinforced over the years when they replay them on TV from time to time. So the TV picture gets fixed in my brain, and becomes more real than the real event, which then somehow detaches me from the whole experience of having run the race in the first place. I know, it's very strange. Anyway, I find myself thinking when I see an old clip, *Oh yeah, I remember that race.* But what I'm really saying is that I remember the TV image, not the actual race itself. Do you know what I mean?

Yeah, it's like how imitations of things become the originals for us, like preferring concentrated orange juice to freshly squeezed.

There are very few races I can sit here with you and describe step by step. That Emsley Carr Mile we've been talking about, that's one. But most of my other races are only familiar to me because of TV. Now in my role as a sports commentator, I go back to these major events like the world championships and Olympics and I find that old memories sometimes hit me about how I felt or what I thought when it was me out there on the track. But it's interesting how I'm completely dispassionate about some of my old races, while others really stir me up and get my emotions going.

Is your mile world record one of those old races that stirs you up?

It is, because that was one of the most important races of my career. I think if I had gone through my whole career and not done that it would have been a huge disappointment. Especially so as a Brit because . . .

Here we are back to the tradition thing?

That's right, because to be a world-class miler and to be British, but to have never held the mile world record would have been a real letdown for me. I guess that's the expectation of success you were asking me about earlier. But did that become a problem or a burden? Again, I don't think so. I got more satisfaction and joy out of breaking the mile world record than anything else I ever did. And part of it was just because people knew what it meant. If I met an American on the street and he asked me my best mile time and I said, 3:46, it brought out a reaction. If I said, but I also ran 3:29 for 1500 meters it wouldn't mean anything to him. Right there that tells you why the mile matters and why it'll always be around.

So for you there was definitely a difference between running a mile and running 1500 meters?

In a mile race I always thought, *Okay, I have to run four laps here.* So it was a four-lap race for me. In a 1500 I used to think about getting the first 300 meters out of the way then making it into a three-lap race. The mile can be neatly divided up; it's easier to pace and easier to judge how you're doing. There was something odd about three and three-quarters laps that I could never really get my head around. And I think a lot of fans, at least in Britain, feel the same way. Crowds always like a good mile race, and not just here. When I used to run the Dream Mile in Oslo the place would go nuts for all four laps. The mile just falls neatly into our psyche, I think. In a way, I suppose it's the perfect event.

Photo courtesy of Mike Barnow

# Sport's Answer

## JAMA ADEN
### (Somalia)

**First sub-4:** July 19, 1983, 3:56.82, Toronto
**Personal best:** 3:56.82
**Total sub-4s:** 11

*George Orwell once referred to sport as "War minus the bullets." He said this follow-
ing World War II, when across Eastern Europe and the United States muscular
strength and coordination were beginning to fuse with economic viability to form a
dynamic relationship among sport, power, and ideology. Orwell admonished sport's
manipulative nature and denied games any sort of carefree, innocent charter. To Orwell
organized play was nothing less than a tool of sporting nationalism and corporate cap-
italism.*

*We need to look no farther than the shooting of 11 Israeli athletes by Palestinian
terrorists at the 1972 Munich Olympics, or the worldwide sporting embargo placed on
South Africa when apartheid still ruled that land, to see that politics have always been
rife across our playing fields. Other critics have expressed sentiments similar to Orwell.
The sociologist Harry Edwards accused American professional sport franchises of prac-*

*ticing institutional racism, and John Hoberman detailed through a careful historical analysis the use of underhanded tactics by athletes over the last century.*

*But sport also holds the influence to do good: the athlete as modest, moderate, and well balanced. This was the ideal Roger Bannister strove to achieve when he first broke four minutes for the mile. Sport can become an instrument of hope and satisfaction; we long for stories that suggest a positive change. And we certainly recoil at sport's ugly side: brawls, players' strikes, drug allegations. The athlete's unheroic act—driving drunk, refusing to sign an autograph for a child—forever disappoints us. We place trust in sport's character-building properties and expect players of all games to display honor, courage, and moral strength. More than anything else, perhaps, we want sport to affect us for the better. We want sport to enhance our lives and set us on a path toward salvation.*

Jama, you were the first Somalian to break four minutes for a mile. Why do you think it took until 1983 for that to happen?

The mile in my country, Jim, is in many ways a nonevent. That has always been so. No one in Somalia knows exactly what a mile is, or where it comes from. They know the 1500 meters mostly. As a boy I had never heard of the mile. Maybe just a few stories only. But after I broke four minutes, I went back to the capital of Somalia, Mogadishu, to organize a mile race, the first one ever in Somalia, and everyone was asking me, *What's a mile? What's a mile?*

What did you tell them?

It's hard to explain, *What's a mile.* Because in Somalia everyone uses the metric system. No one travels a mile, or sees road signs marked in miles. I could tell them the great stories and rivalries of the mile, and the history and importance of four minutes. Like Roger Bannister, Jim Ryun, Sebastian Coe, and Steve Ovett; or the Wanamaker Mile at the Milrose Games in Madison Square Garden. They had never heard of such legends and traditions.

How did those legends and traditions you just mentioned become something you learned and understood?

Until I went to the United States for the first time I didn't know about the value of four minutes for a mile. I went to college in New Jersey when I was 17, to Fairleigh Dickinson University, and the coaches and my teammates were talking about the mile. They talked about the mile all the time. Much more than any other event, including the 1500 meters. Everyone was saying, *Mile, mile, mile, that's the best event, the most important event. Especially to be under four minutes.* But I was originally an 800-meter runner so I didn't understand what they meant by the mile. Soon, though, I came to agree with them: The mile is the best event, the most interesting event.

How did you reach that conclusion?

First of all, and to me most important of all, there was great excitement around the mile. Especially on the East Coast of America where there were big indoor mile races in Madison Square Garden, Boston, and the Meadowlands Arena in New Jersey. The crowds, sometimes more than 10,000, went crazy for the mile. And the top, top guys always ran the mile: Eamonn Coghlan, Steve Scott, John Walker, Marcus O'Sullivan. In Europe, too, I saw that during the summer there was The Dream Mile at the Bislett Games in Oslo where Steve Cram and Said Aouita had so many close races. All of that atmosphere and hype affected me. It affected me very much. You see, Jim, my philosophy as a runner was always do the big things, the important events, the big races. And that was the mile. Why bother doing something unless people care about it and are interested? There is no point if other people don't think it's important; otherwise they won't appreciate and respect who you are and what you are doing. I believe it's important to have the feeling in life of doing a worthwhile job. It's important for me, at least. So I think the mile really became an American habit that I learned to love. Even today, although my running career is over, I care the most about the mile. I study the mile results first whenever I see a track meet.

Were there any milers you particularly admired and looked up to?

Yes, definitely, Filbert Bayi, from Tanzania. His mile world record in Kingston, Jamaica, was a very, very famous and exciting race for me. He beat all the top guys from America and Europe to become the first African to hold the mile world record. Later he became my friend, and we used to talk about the mile and running a fast mile. He loved the mile, more than any other distance. All the milers I mentioned before became my friends: Eamonn, Steve Scott, Marcus, Aouita . . . They are great, great guys. Good people who I like very much. And even today, although none of us are still running, we talk about the mile. John Walker talks about his 3:49 world record, Eamonn talks about his 3:49 indoor mile, and Marcus and Steve Scott talk about how many sub-four-minute miles they have run. So the mile for all of us is very important. For me the mile was also my life: I lived in America as a miler and a student. Always it was the mile that suited my personality. You see, I like people and being around exciting things. The mile was the perfect event for me. If something is too quiet or boring I don't want to do it.  ·

What events led to you coming to America for college?

I have to say one person, Mal Whitfield. It was Mal Whitfield who got me my scholarship. You know who Mal is, right? A great American half-miler who won the Olympic gold medal in 1948 and 1952. He also held the 800-meter world record, and he worked for the American State Department in Africa when his running career was over. It was Mal Whitfield who noticed my talent and my excitement for sport when I was a boy running in Somalia. He saw my enthusiasm to improve my life; he believed I would be a good sporting ambassador for Somalia and help other Somalians through running. That's why today I say, *Thank God for Mal Whitfield;* I say it many times, *Thank God for Mal Whitfield,* because Mal Whitfield saved my life. Ever since he first saw me run he promised me I could get a scholarship to America. But I never knew for sure if I could believe him, or if he was just saying that to motivate me about running. But my Somalian friends who could speak English said it was true: It was a fact that he was going to get me a scholarship. And the day I graduated from high school I got a phone call from the United States embassy in Mogadishu. They had all my visas and paperwork to go to America, including my plane ticket. That was one of the most happy days of my life.

What do you mean, Mal Whitfield saved your life?

If I hadn't left Somalia for running I'm sure I would be dead now. Yes, I'm very certain of that. The political conditions at that time, in 1980, weren't so bad, but they were getting worse and worse day by day. Then everything became so, so horrible. And many bad things began to happen. Today my older brother is dead, and all my friends and colleagues are dead, too, or blind, or seriously injured. There have been so many years of civil war and unrest. Somalia is not even so much a country anymore. At least, it's not a place I recognize or can call home. What a terrible, terrible situation. That's why, *Thank God for Mal Whitfield*. That's all I can say. If it wasn't for him getting me out of Somalia when he did only the worst could have happened. That's a fact I believe with all my heart.

Have you been back to Somalia recently?

No, and anyway that's practically impossible. The wars, the poverty, there is no way I can live there or even visit. It's too unstable. I have my own family and my own responsibilities to take care of . . . my wife, my two little girls, a new baby boy. In Somalia that would be impossible; I couldn't support them; I couldn't make a living and have a safe life. I visited there five years ago for my brother's funeral and it was horrible. I saw many people in such bad shape. I was upset all the time and I could only drink milk. I ate nothing; I couldn't sleep; I couldn't think. I had to leave as soon as possible, after only five days. But it's my dream to return to Somalia and become national running coach. I know I can help other young Somalians to have a better life through running. But now the time is not right. In fact, before conditions got very, very serious I helped many guys get out and come to universities in America to run for a scholarship and earn an education. I was the first Somalian runner to get a college scholarship. I believe I enabled others to do the same. For example, Abdi Bile, who later became 1500-meter world champion for Somalia in Rome in 1987. Our first and only world champion in track and field. He broke all my national records, including the mile. I also asked my father, "Can anyone else in the family be a good runner?" And he said, "Ibrahim," my youngest brother. So I got him to come to America. He went to high school and college there. Now he lives in New Mexico and is even a United States citizen. He just broke my family record for the mile, by the way. He ran 3:55 two weeks ago. I was so, so pleased for him even if it means losing my record.

What were some of the challenges you faced when you left Somalia and went to America?

Well, I was very scared. But also very happy. I didn't speak any English and I knew studying at the university and learning the culture was going to be difficult. But I was determined to work as hard as possible. It was an opportunity I had to take. You see, I was determined to make my standard of living better. That was always my dream. And I knew that the best chance to improve my life was through sport, especially to get to America for an education and a job. Because through my family there was no opportunity to do better. My father ran a small grocery store and it was okay, but we only ever had enough to get by. We never had anything extra. As a boy I hoped to be a hero for my family and my country and do something important to help everyone. In Somalia that happens easiest if you are a sportsman. Being good in sport, more than being good in academics, is a way to get ahead. And for me it had to be running because I wasn't that good at football [soccer]. I was only a reserve on my local team, and I didn't like being on the sidelines. On weekends when my friends would go to Mogadishu for a football tournament and I'd be left back in the village I felt lonely and unimportant. That wasn't good, either. I wanted to be part of something, too, and to be good at something; I wanted to be a winner, so I began running. I began by running with my neighbor who was a very dedicated football player and did drills and sprints for conditioning to improve his football. He all the time asked me to run with him because he knew I was fast. And by running with him I began to get faster and in shape. Then in school one day there was a 400-meter race and I won. Soon after that, I became junior champion for Somalia at 400 meters. And a few years later, when I was 16, I moved up to the 800 and ran 1:50 at the Arab Scholastic Games. That was where Mal Whitfield saw me and told me that I could be a great runner. He was a super, super motivator. The best, Jim, the best. He got me to believe in my ability and talent and that I could keep winning races. That was all I needed to hear to decide that I was a runner, and that I would be serious about my running and try my hardest to run well. I knew then that I would have many good challenges as a runner. But I always liked to challenge myself to become the best I could be. I wasn't afraid of a challenge, and I'm still not today.

Do you remember your earliest running ambitions?

I had the dream to win an Olympic medal, of course. That's the ultimate challenge as a runner, and I liked to set myself the highest standards and expectations. Racing was very exciting to me. Especially to try to win. That was what I loved most about sport: winning. I used to love the butterflies in my stomach before the start of a race, and the atmosphere of an important and hard race. I would start to feel the atmosphere when I was warming up, and that made me think about not losing. When there was a big occasion with a crowd and the best runners in the field, that was when I did my best. I would say I am a very emotional person, so when there was a buzz and hype around an event I got the best result from myself. Many times I ran above my ability and my fitness because I was so pumped up. Although sometimes, I ran badly even though I was in good shape. Maybe I wasn't mentally ready, or feeling a strong belief in myself, or in the occasion, or importance of the race? Anyway, I liked the mile so much and decided to become a miler because it had the best atmosphere.

You said earlier that you were originally an 800-meter runner, so when did you make the transition to the mile?

In 1981, after I was in America for one year, I ran my first mile, the Fifth Avenue Mile in New York City. I ran 4:04, which I thought was okay. Then people were encouraging me to become a miler. Especially because of my skinny build. The next year, 1982, I ran another road mile, in Jersey City, and I ran 3:59.99. I thought, *Hey, I broke four minutes.* I was thrilled. Of course, I knew that it didn't count for real because it was on the road not a track, but still I was very happy. After that, breaking four minutes became a big, big, goal for me. I was even running 1500s on the track and converting my time up to the mile by adding 17 seconds. I didn't care what my 1500 times were, only the mile. When I ran 3:42 for 1500 meters I knew I was close to four minutes and that breaking it would be possible. At that point I believed it was just a matter of time before I did it.

So a four minute mile was never a barrier in your mind?

No, not at all. Once I became determined I was sure I could do it. I knew I just needed to get into the right race at the right pace. For example, I ran 4:01 and even four-flat a couple of times because the pace was too slow at the beginning.

Was there anything about the mile that worried you or frightened you?

The third lap was hard for me. I had a fear of the pain of that lap. The first two laps always went very fast, but then came the third lap. Oh, my chest and legs began to feel bad, like a burning or something. Also, I didn't like uneven races, or races where there were changes in speed from slow to fast. In an 800, for example, it's usually just the one pace right from the start: hard all the way. The mile, though, can be different, and require more tactics. I'd say I ran the mile best when every lap was even and at a steady pace, like around 59 or 58 seconds. Then running felt natural and relaxed to me. Time would pass quickly; I'd have a feeling of floating or cruising. And I could settle in and run comfortably. I remember talking to Filbert Bayi about this and he said that was the African way to run a mile: even and steady from the gun. He thought African runners were bad at waiting around for a kick, but good at running up front. And that was definitely true for me.

So you didn't mind leading a race or pushing the pace from the front?

I was always willing to make a race go. Like in my first sub-four-minute mile when I moved to the lead after the second lap to keep the pace going fast. I can remember that very clearly. I felt the pace begin to slow down after two laps and I didn't want that to happen. Everything was going so well. We had passed the half mile in 1:56 and I felt great. I wasn't tired at all. And after I heard, 1:56, I became very, very excited. I was repeating to myself, *This is it. This is your lifetime opportunity to break four minutes for real, not like on the road.* I knew this was my big chance, and that I had to keep going. *Keep going,* I said to myself over and over. So I took the lead, and as soon as I hit the front I knew I was going to break four minutes.

How did you know?

I just felt too good; my stride was easy and flowing. There was no way I was going to die or slow down so much that I would run over four minutes. No way.

And your reaction when you broke four minutes?

I was thrilled to death. To run 3:56 for my first time under four minutes, My goodness, it felt great. I was very, very happy. And the meet director that day, Paul Geis, he was hugging me and saying, "Look what you did. Look what you did." It meant so much to me. Honestly, I felt like a real miler after that.

Did you call your parents or anyone else in Somalia to tell them what you had done?

There was no reason to call anyone in Somalia. I called other friends in America, though. Back home a 3:56 mile wouldn't have been something my parents could understand. They wouldn't know the value of it.

Did that make you sad, not to be able to share such a big achievement with your family?

No, because I knew why they didn't understand. It wasn't that they didn't care about me or my running. There was just no tradition of the mile for them to understand 3:56. So that's fine, I accepted that. How can they celebrate something that has no meaning in Somalia? But that didn't stop me from being happy. I was very proud to become a sub-four-minute miler, the first one from my country. That night I couldn't sleep I was so happy and excited. I was with my American running friends, and other guys who were in the race . . . Richard O'Flynn from Ireland, Sosthenes Bitok from Kenya. We were celebrating all night and having so much fun. It was a great, great feeling. And you know, I thought it was going to be just the start of faster and faster mile races for me. But it's strange because that was my fastest mile ever, that first one under four minutes.

Why do you think that was?

I'm not sure, but at some stage later on in my running career I think I lost my killer instinct. Or at least I lost some belief in myself. After two years, when I didn't run any faster than my 3:56 from 1983, I was going to meets in America or Europe and being put into the B races. I began to feel like a second-class runner because I wasn't running the featured races. And that was bad for me. The B races had no atmosphere or big-name runners. Sometimes the crowd didn't even watch. It was hard for me to get excited and do my best in that situation. And I would just run without a lot of confidence or motivation. There was a time when I even thought of quitting because not improving was so frustrating for me. I very quickly began to lose hope in myself and my future as a runner.

Do you think your despair about your future as a runner at that time could have been linked to events back home and worsening conditions in Somalia?

Maybe. Those were hard years in the middle 1980s for me, my family, and my country. I was away from Somalia and I would see all the death and destruction from back home on television. And I'd wonder, *What's really happening? Why is everything so crazy and bad?* I was constantly worried about the people I knew and loved. It was a scary time and a sad time.

But you didn't quit running, did you? You continued racing through all that turmoil.

I did, I know. And I have to say it was because of the friends I had made through running that I decided not to quit. When I honestly thought about quitting, I asked myself, *What else am I going to do if I don't run?* My life was traveling to races and being with my friends. So back I went to run more races.

And you never regretted that decision?

No, because after all running saved my life. So how could I ever feel bitter about my results or anything in my life associated with running? I'm alive today and life is good after all.

# Promise

## MARTIN HEMSLEY
### (United States)

First sub-4: May 17, 1986, 3:59.70, Eugene, Oregon
Personal best: 3:59.70
Total sub-4s: 1

$N$*ow, this is one I can say I participated in. And not just in some emotionally supportive way, like a fan who paints his face or boasts loudly when ever possible, "We did it. We beat them." After all, sport largely survives and perpetuates itself through its fans: Rooters establish the standards that young athletes dream to achieve. It's rare, however, when we can do anything more concrete than wear our team's colors on game day, or buy the season in review video every Christmas. The glory we bask in as fans is refracted; it barely touches us—although the sentiments of success can run deep, as if we had actually done the work ourselves.*

*A miler's work is sternest through autumn and winter. The months of cold-weather training over dark paths buoyed only by the anticipation of spring and the promise of faster times—a sub-four-minute mile perhaps. Marty's autumn and winter of 1985-86 was made easier, though. He had me by his side; we were training partners in New York, and together we managed our long runs and track intervals without concern or hesitation. At the same time, progress for one of us meant progress for the other. Except on one ocassion when Marty did something I didn't recognize in myself. We were moving through a series of steep hill repetitions when he sudennly rose off the ground. From beside my shoulder in the middle of one stride, he seemed to advance five paces in the next. He was gone, away out front. And I knew it was more than a case of him just having a good day. I had to admit that he possessed an element of strength missing in me.*

*To acknowledge an inadequacy in ourselves following the comparison to another can sometimes leave a lingering sting that sours into jealously. But Marty's ways as a runner were too humble and unassuming. His demeanor sparked admiration, not rivalry. In his company, I was pleased to take a step back.*

*Marty left for Eugene, Oregon, that March full of quality work. Through the spring he improved steadily; week by week he lowered his times. He called me in New York that May 17 night, and I basked wholly and justifiably in what he had done.* We did it, Marty. We broke four minutes, *I said to myself.*

Running, it has to be said, Marty, is somewhat of a minority sport in America, so why weren't you, for example, a baseball player?

I was, to a degree. Like most kids I played Little League, and in my neighborhood in the Bronx we were always out on the street playing touch football or stickball . . . stuff like that. But beyond any influence the Yankees or Mets had on me, there was one sporting moment that really affected me growing up. Even today I remember it so clearly: the 1972 Olympics.

What was it about those Olympics that captured your imagination?

The 800 meters and Dave Wottle's gold medal.

Not the 1500 meters?

Sure, I remember Jim Ryun falling in the 1500 meters, and how he was supposed to win. And there he was walking off the track in tears . . . that was definitely a big deal. But more than anyone else it was Wottle who impressed me: how he came from last place with 200 meters to go to pick off the Soviet runner at the line. I thought that was so cool . . . to have a giant kick like that and then to nail the Soviet guy at the tape. Those were pretty nationalistic times in America with lots of USSR versus USA propaganda floating around. As a kid I suppose I was caught up in that to an extent. Anyway, that moment, Wottle winning, really sparked my interest in running. He looked incredible charging down the track, passing everyone, and I thought if I could do that myself one day, maybe even in the Olympics, that would be something. Actually, my friends and I organized our own Olympics out on the street that summer. We had boxing, wrestling, and the marathon. We used giant oversized gloves, made a ring, and punched each other around. It was hilarious. For the marathon, I remember, I ran up and down the block against another kid for God only knows how many times until we finally decided it was the last lap . . . then he sprinted away and outkicked me. But he was three years older, so I thought I had done all right.

After the '72 Olympics, did you start acting like a runner and training and racing?

No, no, no. I was only nine years old then, and age-group running for some reason had a bad reputation. Everyone thought it would burn you out. I was content to wait until high school. But I lived near Van Cortlandt Park, which was where all the New York City cross-country meets were held, and I used to walk down there by myself on Saturdays to watch the races.

So you were actually a fan before you began running yourself.

I was. Although I was starting to get a reputation in my neighborhood as a runner. In the sixth grade, which would have been, let's see . . . 1974, my class had a mile race and a quarter-mile race and I won them both.

And at this point, had you already decided that the half-mile and mile were going to be your events?

Yeah, that kind of happened without too much thought or knowledge of the sport. I suppose those events just appealed to me somehow.

In what other ways did you carry forward your interest in running following the '72 Olympics?

Well, *Sports Illustrated* had articles on track occasionally, and I read all of them. The newspapers carried lots of results, too. I remember reading about Steve Prefontaine's death in 1975 and being really aware of what he had done for American distance running. But even before that, in 1974, I bought the New York State High School Track Yearbook, which listed all the top performances in every event by New York high school runners. And I remember being really impressed by this one runner, Mark Belger, from Long Island, who was the best half-miler in New York and the nation. I used to flip through that book a lot and look at all the names and times and different schools.

Were you imagining seeing your own name in that book someday?

I suppose so. I was pretty much into the whole New York high school running scene. I could name all the best local runners, and which schools had the best teams. Also, my older brother was one of the top milers in New York City. I followed running even more closely than he did, although he was actually on a team and I wasn't even in high school yet.

Did you share your early ambitions about wanting to be a great runner with anyone?

No, not at all. That wasn't the way I did things. I preferred to keep all of that stuff to myself. Running was like "My Thing." I had my running friends and all that, but I had friends outside of running, too. I didn't need to go around talking about running to everyone all the time. But running did give me a sense of belonging. I loved the community aspect of it, and socializing with other runners. To some degree, I liked that stuff the most. However, people in my neighborhood, probably because of my brother's success, did have expectations of me as a runner. And in some ways that was hard to live up to because I didn't do anything extraordinary in my first three years of high school.

Did that worry you, the fact that you didn't make an immediate impact as a runner?

I have to say that I was pretty patient with myself, or maybe *realistic* is a better word. You see, I was small as a freshman, and some kids I was racing against were incredibly mature. You know, with big muscles . . . even shaving. I figured I'd grow eventually. As it turned out, though, I didn't really do anything all that decent until my senior year, which was a little disappointing, I suppose. Junior year my best 800 was 2:02, and my best mile was 4:42. Going into my senior year, though, I set goals of 1:55 and 4:15.

Were those goals or ultimatums?

Goals. I wasn't going to give up that easily.

Did you do anything special in terms of your preparation or race strategy in order to reach those goals your senior year?

That summer I probably ran more than I ever had before. I got hold of a training program from one of the local colleges and followed that. It was a lot of long slow distance, which was what everyone did back then, especially as a way to prepare for the mile. Still, I only had a mediocre cross-country season, which was again kind of disappointing. But during indoor track I started to run better, although I wasn't close to where I thought I should've been.

Beyond your immediate goal of 4:15 for the mile, were you thinking at this point about bigger things, for example breaking four minutes?

Well, yes and no about the four-minute thing. To be honest, four minutes wasn't where my sights were aimed. Maybe it sounds a bit naive or over ambitious now, but I was thinking more about breaking the mile world record. I didn't see myself as having limits but rather lots of promise. And thankfully, over the last couple of weeks of my senior year I had somewhat of a breakthrough when I won the New York City Catholic High Schools Championship in the 800 in 1:57. Then in my first year of college I ran 1:53 and 4:12, and because I was only 18 years old, which is how old a lot of guys are in their senior year of high school, I thought I was on target to keep progressing to the level I wanted to reach.

So you were always optimistic about your results and your future as a runner?

Yeah, why not. I had lots of time to improve.

What other goals did you set for yourself early in your career?

I wanted to qualify for events like the Junior Nationals, and the National Collegiate Championships. Really, though, I just wanted to concentrate on winning races and lowering my times every year. But in 1984, while running for the University of Oregon, four minutes did become a goal for me. In Eugene, four minutes was a big deal. Obviously a lot of guys focused on it because of the great meets they put on there and the long tradition of Oregon milers. That year, in fact, I ran 4:01 in a local meet that featured most of the top guys. The stadium was packed, and that was a big improvement for me, like six or seven seconds.

Had you started that race with specific designs on breaking four minutes?

I can't recall, quite honestly. I don't think so, though. I was more or less just happy to be in the race. And I was only thinking about doing my best and not embarrassing myself. But I do remember looking up at the scoreboard clock with a lap to go, and it said, 3:02. And I thought to myself, *Hey, I can get under four.*

What happened next?

Well, we were all bunched up in a pack and I was toward the back. But I felt good, not like I was struggling to hang on. Then the pace picked up and down the backstretch everybody started to string out. I finished seventh, and when I saw that the winner had run 3:58 I knew I must have done okay because I wasn't that far behind, maybe 25 yards. Then one of the guys I trained with told me that I ran 4:01. That stunned me a bit, I must admit. I was pleased, though, to finally run what was considered by most people to be a decent time. Actually, a lot of guys on the team couldn't believe I had run that fast because I had been struggling in most of my races up to that point. But that had a lot to do with the training system at Oregon, which was based on strength-type work, and I was more used to a speed program. So I was getting used to that at the same time. But Eugene was such a great place to live and train. There weren't too many places in America back then where you could run 4:01 and end up seventh. In fact, there aren't too many places today where that could happen, except maybe Palo Alto. So the depth of talent in Eugene was enormous, and not just from the college runners but from all the postcollegians who lived and trained there, too.

Following that 4:01, four minutes must have seemed like a dead certainty to you?

Yeah, I knew I had it in me. And there were a few more opportunities that year for me to try to do it. But toward the end of May I could feel myself running out of gas. So I decided to stop for the season and build myself up for the year to come.

That would have been 1985. What happened?

I ran faster over the mile and the 1500, but only by a little bit. And actually, it was at the meet where I ran that 4:01 the year before that I really thought I could break four minutes. But I didn't have it that night and so I ran another 4:01.

Was that disappointing?

Yeah, as a whole that entire season was disappointing. But I knew there was always next year.

So what were your 1986 plans regarding breaking four minutes?

All through that winter, which I spent in New York, my training was going really well . . . better than I ever could have expected. But you know that yourself. And my early indoor races indicated that I was in great shape. Then in January I was scheduled to run a mile at Harvard, and I definitely had in mind breaking four minutes. But two days before that race I got food poisoning and that pretty much put an end to my indoor season. But you know, that was just a case of bad luck. So all I could really do was begin preparing for outdoors.

But at this point were you still thinking about breaking the mile world record one day?

Ah, well . . . well, my ideas in that regard were changing. I still did think that I could run fast and possibly make an impact on the national scene, but the world record? Put it this way: After I saw Steve Cram run 3:46 to set a new world record in 1985 and right afterward they stuck a microphone in his face and he was fine, I started to think that maybe I wasn't going to be able to do that.

Why? What did you see as your main limitation?

Speed and strength. Here was a guy [Cram] who could run 1:42 for 800 meters. I just didn't have that kind of talent and power. I was a 51-second quarter-miler. Also, how many guys only ran 4:30 for a mile in high school but ended up breaking four minutes? Not a lot. So, yeah, I had limitations.

Was that difficult for you to face?

Well, it was pretty damn sobering watching how easily Cram ran 3:46. But don't get me wrong, I was still excited to continue to try to win races and run faster times. Not only that, like I said before, I always saw running as something much bigger in my life. Sure there were frustrating moments and disappointing times, but that's the same with anything. As a runner, I had great fun. I traveled, I met interesting people all over the world, and I made great friends that I still have today.

Indeed, you would run faster. Because in the spring of 1986, you went back to Eugene and . . .

That's right, I went back to Eugene, got a few good early-season races under my belt, and then broke four minutes.

Tell me about that day.

The race was at about 8:30 at night, so during the morning and afternoon I just relaxed. Maybe I watched some television, or took a nap, I can't really remember. When the race started I felt good, and my splits were dead even on 60 for the first three laps: 60, 2:00, 3:00. I was also in good position the whole way, maybe third or fourth. And with a lap to go I was telling myself, *Okay, you're right there. Stay in it.* Then the leader took off with 300 yards left and totally spread out the field. And at this point all I could really do was keep running my hardest. Down the backstretch for the last time I knew I was running well, but I wasn't sure how well. That week's training had been kind of tough so my legs were a little tired; I didn't have a good gauge of myself as fresh and totally on top of my game. Even with half a lap remaining, I didn't know if I would be under four. I just didn't feel like I was running particularly fast. But I didn't feel like I was running slow, either; there was definitely some labor involved, though. But I kept digging because I knew it would be close, and the crowd was making a lot of noise, too, because in the lead was a guy on the Oregon team. Finally, when I crossed the finish line I looked straight over at a friend who was on the side of the track with a stopwatch in his hands and he was nodding his head and grinning. So I immediately knew that I had broken four minutes. And I was like, *All right, I finally did it.* Which was a really good feeling. Later I called home and gave my parents the news and they were really pleased. Then I called you. And the next day I called everyone else in my family. That night was also a lot of fun. I was out at different bars and parties and just celebrating a big day with all my Eugene friends.

Does the fact that you're a sub-four-minute-miler come up in your life today at all?

In business it comes up all the time. Somehow people find out that I ran a sub-four-minute mile and then they ask me about it. Older people, especially, because they know the history of Roger Bannister and what four minutes meant as a barrier and a landmark achievement. Sometimes it's uncomfortable for me when people bring it up because they don't know how four minutes fits into the larger scheme of track. They think because I broke four minutes I must have run in the Olympics and been some superstar. But that just says something about people's knowledge of track.

There are only a few names and events, like Bannister or Jesse Owens, that everyone knows about.

Why do you think the four-minute mile is part of people's general sports knowledge?

It's clear; it's easy to understand; it gets hyped up in the papers. People can relate to a mile. After all, four laps in four minutes; what can be simpler than that?

Finally, Marty, any feelings about breaking four just once?

Well, when I did it I certainly didn't think it would be my only time. My expectations were higher. To a detached observer it might appear I had achieved a level of satisfaction, but that was never my thinking. I always thought I would be much better.

Photo by Stuart Franklin

# Running National

## WILLIAM TANUI
### (Kenya)

First sub-4: March 4, 1992, 3:56.87, San Sebastian, Spain
Personal best: 3:50.57
Total sub-4s: 22

*R*unning *shoes litter the entranceway, pairs and pairs of them; bags branded with Puma, Nike, and Adidas and stuffed with sweatpants, T-shirts, towels, and jackets line the hallway. I step carefully, targeting the few clear spots of wooden floor. Sweet cooking smells, onion with ginger, swirl above me; there aren't nearly enough chairs for everyone, so most stand, or mill about and chat easily. The singsong foreign tones rest easily on my mind; words string into melodies. The tall one who greeted me at the door encourages me to follow him inside. "So cold outside, yes?" he says. Followed by, "I am William." His strong handshake and smart white smile shrink the gap between us. And with his hand over mine and our palms kissing, I think about never letting go. William manages to secure a space in the corner where we can talk; I trail in the path he clears.*

*I've heard stories about this famous London address, the place so many Kenyan runners call home as they transit to and from races across Europe. "It's cross-country season now. There are good money races in Spain and Italy," William tells me. This is one hub of the Kim McDonald Sports Management Agency. But it feels more like I've walked into the middle of a big family at dinnertime, not a profitable enterprise.*

*I can't imagine how many great runners I must be among. I know the credentials of the man before me, but who else is here? I try to detect who's who. Is that. . . ? And over there, is that. . . ? Then I remember, I have business to conduct. I am curious, though. Where does everyone sleep? Who's racing next? How does everyone find his way here, and then home again? But these are questions for another story. It's certainly true that running is business today. For the Kenyans it means learning to travel, to speak with writers, and to race set distances; the money they earn stretches far at home. Their time through London is short, after all. And from the mood here tonight, it's obvious that they are all both here and far away.*

William, could you tell me how you became aware of the mile as a track event?

In primary school, when I was 10, I remember one day the teacher said we have to run a mile. *What's a mile?* I thought. I didn't know except that it was four laps of the track. The word *mile,* it was new to me and didn't really mean anything. In Kenya we practiced the metric system, you see. Even many years after that I didn't know much about the mile. I was in the army running and we ran the 1500 meters only. The mile was still just a four lap race to me, different, and most importantly longer than the 1500. For years that was all I knew about the mile. But that's typical in Kenya. Even today young runners only try 1500 meters. It's not until we go to Europe or America that mile races become something usual for us.

Do you remember your first mile race?

It was 1989, in Britain, the south. That was the first time it was official and timed. I ran 4:01.

How did that race feel?

Oh, hard. It felt very, very long to me.

And what did you think of your time, 4:01?

I knew it was okay, but only okay. I knew if you can break four minutes, though, you are better.

How did you learn that?

The other Kenyans who were already over here running said. Joseph Chesire, he told me, "Break four minutes when you run the mile. The English people, they like that. And then you are not a bad runner." So I decided that is what I have to do in my next mile race, break four minutes.

And did you?

No. It was hard, and took longer than I thought, three years. This was very frustrating to me because I gave myself such pressure to break four minutes. I knew that if I wanted to be able to consider myself an okay runner I have to do it. I was putting in a lot of effort and training hard to break four minutes. There was even a time when I think maybe it's impossible for me.

What do you think made breaking four minutes so hard for you?

The last lap was very hard. Mentally it gave me so much trouble. I was used to the 1500 and thinking, *Ah, only 300 meters to go.* This was after the three-quarters. But with the mile there is still a whole lap left after the three-quarters. To me that was very tiring. And I think it's the same for most Kenyans. It felt like such a long way . . . the finish never came, and I would ask myself, *Where is the finish?*

But of course, you eventually did break four minutes, and by a lot, more than three seconds all at once. Do you remember that race?

That was a joyous day. It was in Spain and I was in the race with Noureddine Morceli {former mile world-record holder from Algeria}. I knew he could pull me to a fast time. I was only thinking, *Stay close to Morceli, follow him, and you'll get your four minutes.* I felt good energy that day, and with

half a lap left I was still sprinting and running hard but also feeling easy. I
knew then that I would break four minutes. Soon afterward I saw my time
and thought, *Finally, I have done it.* And then my next thought was, *I'm sure
now I can run even faster.*

Did everyone congratulate you for breaking four minutes?

For most of my countrymen it was a surprise because at the time I was
running mostly 800s. They couldn't believe it. They say to me, "Oh,
William, now you are miler, too." There was laughing and joking. A lot of
happiness. And a big relief for me to get past that standard finally.

What about any reaction from home? Did you call anyone in Kenya to say
that you had broken four minutes?

No, no, no. People in Kenya aren't interested in whether a person just runs
a new best time. There is no reaction. It is not important. They only care if
someone sets a new world record or something like that. This is what the
Kenyan people have become used to because of all our recent success and
winning.

Why are Kenyans such good distance runners?

It's not just the genes or special muscles in our legs like some Americans
and Europeans think. We work very hard, most days training three times,
and our diet is healthy and natural. Also, employment is a big problem in
Kenya. Many people have a terrible standard of living. If someone runs a race
in America and wins $1,000 that is 70,000 Kenyan shillings. A military offi-
cer needs one year to earn that much. So improving our lifestyle is also a
motivating factor.

How important is it for you to be a "Kenyan" runner, not just William
Tanui the runner?

I always trained in a group back in Kenya, which was great support. I had
no personal coach or direct advice from anyone. I learned about running from

the group—how fast to go, when to rest, and different tactics. The group was around 15 guys, all middle-distance runners, and we did the same workouts together. That gives us the motivation and competition. And we like to train together. You see here tonight in the house we like to be together. As Kenyans we win and lose together.

Is that *harambee*?

Ah, you know *harambee*. Yes, it's an important Kenyan word that means "pulling together as a group." We believe in Kenya that nothing is achievable alone. A man cannot build a house by himself; neither can he become a world champion runner. Results are not so personal to us like in America and Europe. When we train with each other we don't try to beat somebody else as our goal. In the group we work harder together by always trying to follow the fastest. I am a Kenyan runner first and most important. Like when I was the pacesetter for the last mile world record in Rome [the Moroccan Hicham El Guerrouj's current record, 3:43.13, July 7, 1999] it was my joy to help El Guerrouj and Noah [Noah Ngeny from Kenya, who placed second and also ran under the previous record]. I was so excited to lead and run for them and make a new record. Especially when the British runners Coe, Ovett, and Cram had the mile record for so many years. We as Africans wanted the record for us. I only hope now that someday a Kenyan runner will hold the mile record. It has not happened yet. But soon it will.

Who were the runners you grew up admiring?

I would listen to races from Europe and America on the radio and cheer for Kipchoge Keino and Mike Boit. They were so great and famous. I was proud they were from my country. Our teachers in school would tell us about them and the records they broke—1500 meters, steeplechase. There was one day after hearing about a new record for Mike Boit that I decided, *I will try and run as fast as them.* I knew it would take time, but as long as I kept progressing I thought I could do it.

So was it because of Keino and Boit that you began running?

It was my lifestyle and upbringing in the village that I began running. My school was 3 miles away. There were no buses. I ran in the morning to school, I ran back home for lunch, I ran back to school for the afternoon, and finally home again. Then we had a running competition at school, and racing became easy for me because this is what I do every day. And I wouldn't get tired compared to the other kids. For me it was no problem and I could see that for them it was—so you see, not every Kenyan boy is a natural runner. But it was difficult for me to run on a track. That was very hard to adjust to. It didn't feel natural, like running through the country. Because when I'm running to and from school sometimes I stop or walk or have a drink or maybe talk to someone. But when at school they tell us we have to go two or three or even five laps without stopping I think that is very difficult. I didn't like that but I got used to it.

After you became a sub-four-minute miler did it open any doors for you on the international running circuit?

Yes, in certain ways because it gave me confidence and motivation to try running more miles and 1500s. My first sub-four-minute mile was a gateway for me personally, and afterward I began to run even faster for 1500 meters and the mile. Now I could do more at a meeting, not just an 800.

So you learned to like the mile, even the last lap?

Maybe not the last lap, yet. But yes, to me, the mile became interesting: the mix of tactics, the combination of speed and strength. I liked how I had to think about using both.

What's your favorite tactic as a miler?

I like to be in the front and push the pace. Also, when I start to get tired if I am in the front I'm closer to being finished and this doesn't make it seem so hard. If you are in the back you have to speed up when you are getting tired and try to pass people and kick. That takes too much energy. I like the momentum from leading and trying to hold on to the lead.

Was it always your goal when you began running to compete in races around the world?

Kipchoge Keino and Mike Boit were from my same tribe, the Nandi. Everyone was talking about them when they were racing so well. All boys wanted to be like them. They broadcast on the radio any race in the world where Kenyan runners were—Britain, America, Jamaica, Japan. I would then look at the globe in school and think, *It's possible to go all over the world just running? The thing I do every day.* It was amazing to me that it could be that simple. That motivated me to start running harder and harder and training for real. I was curious to see the world but always I knew I would come back to the village. Because like I said before, I am a Kenyan first.

Photo courtesy of Mike Barnow

# Tracks Ahead

## DESMOND ENGLISH
### (Ireland)

**First sub-4: June 25, 1994, 3:58.71, Cork, Ireland**
**Personal best: 3:58.71**
**Total sub-4s: 1**

*T*he geography of a four-minute mile avows an immediate sense of respect. It's a com-
prehensible compression of time and space that sees a man arriving at point B from point
A in an efficient, admirable style. There's also a humanistic dimension to four minutes:
It's an interpretive drama that deposits rich, and often indescribable feelings and memories. "As human beings we run," says John Bale, the British geographer who has studied running's spaces and places for over 25 years, "to understand our various internal
and external landscapes—clocks, emotions, muscles, bones." Running, therefore, maps a
course for one's identity to unfold; and a track, I would argue, presents a highly visible
landmark—a stitch of red, blue, or even green thread sewn through the earth—for this
act to occur. And for obvious reasons tracks can't be triangular, rectangular, or square.
Those shapes, with their hard corners and sharp edges, are cold and dangerous. Rather,
a track's circular, almost oval form has been designed with ease of motion in mind; its
thin white lines and wide spaces in between that wrap around the bend before straight-

*ening out again provide a strong guide forward. But inside the four-minute miler's*
*body, where the mystery of performance lies, blood cells transport oxygen, and lungs*
*inhale and exhale; in effect, every breath becomes a beat, or a journey, or a squeezebox*
*filling and emptying, opening and closing. Or perhaps the direction running entails is*
*more like a spinning top, or a spinning wheel, or a circulating decimal. Or is it a cir-*
*cumflex, a cirrus cloud, or some other circumstance like a change of heart or a newfound*
*narrative of progress and growth?*

Desmond, do you remember how four minutes for a mile became a standard you admired and understood?

I can't really point to an exact moment, or a single image or event, like
reading a book or magazine article, or watching a specific race on television.
I don't know when the idea of four minutes as an important achievement first
coalesced in my head. I think it's just part of our common consciousness or
curriculum . . . at least in Ireland and Britain it is, which are the places that
represent my grounding in so many cultural things like this.

So it's general knowledge, you're saying?

Yes, to a degree. I think we absorb *four minutes for a mile* as part of our
shared human literacy. It becomes a round figure we point to, like a beacon. And I think this almost happens by osmosis. How else can you explain
the four-minute mile's pervasiveness as a sporting icon other than it being
this classic popular culture artifact? I know that sounds a bit contradictory
—classic and popular culture—but the four-minute mile does represent
this lasting but also contemporary benchmark that we immediately associate with athletics. Most people today still think that four minutes remains
the standard for the mile. They aren't aware that it's now, what would I say
. . . sub-3:50.

You don't think four minutes is a respected standard anymore?

As a barrier four minutes still carries tremendous respect from every level
of running community across the world, and among the larger public as well.
It's a general human endeavor, isn't it? An accomplishment that transcends

borders and nationalities, like climbing Mount Everest. And that's certainly not a New Zealand thing just because a New Zealander did it first. Likewise, four minutes, I don't believe, is a British thing just because the first man to do it was British. But the mile is largely invisible from the present racing landscape in Ireland; it has turned into something that is spoken about more than it's seen. That fantastic lore and mystery around Roger Bannister survives in most people's minds as what miling is today. A fast 1500-meter race isn't something the average sports fan can appreciate. Will 3:33 or 3:31 ever replace the existing categories of "running excellence" that people carry around in their heads? As a result, the general understanding of world-class middle-distance running remains four minutes. For example, if I was to run 3:38 for 1500 meters next week and tell my neighbor, it wouldn't mean a thing to him. Whereas if I told him I just ran a mile in 3:58 he'd be immensely impressed, even though it's an inferior mark.

Is it some form of nostalgia that keeps the mile alive?

People definitely have an endearment for the mile . . . or a warm spot they maintain. For instance, whenever a mile's put on the schedule in a European track meet everyone says, *Oh, great, that's interesting.* Whether that's nostalgia and signifies people's longing to return to the past, I don't know. But clearly there's a mystique to the mile that captivates people's imagination.

Do you prefer running the mile to the 1500?

Well, given where I am now with my running, which is clearly sub-elite, I have to contest as many quality 1500-meter races as possible in order to meet standards and qualifying times for championships. And the 1500 is the definitive event to get those marks. So presently, I'm not seeking any mile races. But when I do have the opportunity to run a mile I really look forward to it because it gives me a chance to benchmark myself against history. It's a Corinthian landmark after all. But honestly, running a mile is almost a luxury for me today. I can only afford it when I don't have to worry about standards and selection.

When you do run a mile, do you strategize it differently from a 1500?

Oh, definitely. I see the 1500 as a frenetic event, perhaps more like an 800, and to some extent I feel like I'm racing harder when I run a 1500, and doing everything I can just to hang on. For me, the 1500 has a sense of urgency to it, followed by a snap that represents that last 300 after I've passed three laps. Getting into a good position off the line, for example, seems more important in a 1500. The whole thing just has this intensity about it. Whereas the mile appears calmer to me; I'm still racing, mind you, but I have a sense of being more relaxed, like I'm building and building all the way through it. Maybe that's because the mile is slightly longer, and therefore disturbs the familiar geography of the 1500? At the end of the day, the mile for me is about consistency, regularity, and strength. I'm seeking a clear rhythm and an even tempo: one minute, two minutes, three minutes; what I would call *regular reference points*. The 1500, on the other hand, with its start in one place and its finish in another, is irregular. The mile's like an old friend whose company you only have the odd opportunity to enjoy. And naturally that makes it less threatening. You're not going for a European championship qualifier when you're running a mile, are you? It's more about each individual runner's personal experience; moreover, everyone in the field is cognizant of four minutes and that history. So you're running with tradition on your side, too. Even if you're being beaten in a mile race, you can still think about four minutes. In that way, the mile seems to offer the runner something noble or worthwhile to pursue whatever the circumstance.

How did you gravitate toward the mile as your event?

That's interesting, really, because it's a complete accident that I'm a miler today. Through high school and college I saw myself as an 800-meter runner. I didn't really fancy cross-country as a kid, so that turned me off high volume training and longer races like the mile. Largely I did high-intensity work, and off that ran 1:48, which I suppose was good enough to satisfy my early ambitions. The 800 also felt easy, which I thought meant it must be the right race for me. Then in 1994, I was supposed to run the 800 at Cork City Sports, which is quite a big meeting here in Ireland. But when I arrived at the track and went to check in, the meet organizer told me that I had been bumped from the 800 and put into the mile instead.

Just like that?

Yeah, yeah, I was really annoyed and felt totally disgraced. With the meet director's attitude and the way he gave me the news, it was almost as a total aside. I reckon some big name became available for the 800 at the last minute and they needed space on the track, so I was out. Anyway, when he put me into the mile as a consolation, I was like, "But I'm not trained for the mile. I've trained to run the 800." Basically he just said tough. So I had to deal with it didn't I? And that's what was strange about the whole thing: I seemed to accept this act of fate quite quickly. Sure, I was pissed off initially, but then my attitude became, *Okay, here's an interesting opportunity, let's see what I can make of it.* So in that regard, I felt no pressure whatsoever going into the race. I was totally relaxed and calm. After all, the mile wasn't home territory for me. It was something that I perceived the big boys did like John Walker or Steve Cram, and I was just a visitor or a guest being permitted by pure circumstance to run on this hallowed ground.

Would this have been your first mile ever?

Besides one or two as a schoolkid, yes.

But you had run the 1500 before?

Only a few times, but never seriously. At that time, running the 1500 for me was about having a break from the 800, or something I did early in the season before getting into my real speed work. My best was 3:45, which was nothing spectacular, but off 800 training I felt it was all right. So because I had no deep personal history in the mile, I went into that Cork race thinking, *I'll just run this naturally.* I knew in advance that the pacesetter was set to go through halfway in 1:58, so right away I figured I'd hang off the back. And that's pretty much what I did. I came through the first lap in 60, the second lap in 2:01, and . . .

What were your thoughts halfway?

I felt comfortable and relaxed, believe it or not. I was expecting every step to be very painful, torture almost, but nothing like that was developing at all, which I have to admit was a great surprise and a pleasant relief. Also, because I had started in the back I was beginning to overtake some guys and move up through the field, I was actually gaining confidence as the race progressed. But I was still cautious, of course, because really I had no idea what was waiting for me farther down the track. Then coming into the last lap I was still passing people. It was a big field, close to 18, so there were lots of guys for me to get around and I was almost jumping by them I felt so fresh. Also, for the first time in the race, I was actually getting into the symmetry and balance of the event itself. If you can imagine, the mile took me into its fold, and like I said to you before, because I felt like a visitor out there, I was conscious of remaining quiet. Even though I felt quite strong and energetic coming into the bell lap, I didn't want to be a noisy or obtrusive guest. That would have been rude. Also, part of me was still expecting a rush of pain to rise up any second and cripple me. So every forward step at that point felt like a gift.

What was your three-quarter-mile time?

Bang on three minutes. But I didn't know it at the time. My senses instead were suddenly focused on the moment of the race and gradually building and passing people.

So you weren't cognizant at this point in the race of trying to get under four minutes?

Not at all. I knew I was going all right, but I didn't want to turn cocky or, God forbid, greedy and think about that. The last thing I wanted to do right then was redline it. I became concerned about maintenance instead. I was in this unbelievable mode of concentration that I didn't want to disturb or shatter. Then with 300 to go, I don't know how I did it but I caught the leading bunch, which included Marcus O'Sullivan, who was one of my early running idols, and David Kibet from Kenya, and I was thinking to myself, *Boy, this is really good.* Next I started hearing people shouting my name, which spurred me on even more. I was really rolling at this point, and improving my position even further. Then I did something that struck me as totally sacrosanct, and I couldn't believe I had done it, but I passed Kibet.

Why *sacrosanct?*

Well, here I was just a jumped-up 800-meter runner in my first serious mile race passing a Kenyan, and a 3:51 one no less. *Come on, this isn't right. I shouldn't be doing this,* I was thinking at the time. But I wasn't afraid to do it either. I was just like, *This is bloody great, this is.*

So you were really enjoying yourself out there?

Yeah, I was having a great time, and especially because like I said to you, I wasn't feeling any pain at all. Now with 200 to go, my parents and my cousins and all my mates were going mad from the side of the track. I could hear them clear as day. I think they were just so shocked to see me up near the front, like you would be if you had a bet on a horse who had started with almost no chance. Then with 100 to go I hit the lead . . . amazing really. But it was right after that when I knew I was a visitor to the mile. In about five strides I got hit with the most incredible wave of pain. And guess what happened next? Kibet cruised past me with the most perfect knee lift and relaxed expression I had ever seen in my life. And for the first time, the thought came to me, *Jesus, how am I going to finish this?* I'll tell you, that last straightaway was ugly. It was what this old Irish coach I knew called *acid dancing*. So in the end, I was just trying to get to the line in one piece. And I kept telling myself, *Keep going, keep going.* Then two more guys passed me, and I was like, *Oh, no.* But I managed to hold onto my form somewhat and I finished fourth, which at first felt a bit disappointing, but that quickly passed because, honestly, I was so pleased to have held my own against a group of real milers.

Did your thoughts immediately turn to your time and whether you had broken four minutes?

Strangely enough, they didn't. After I crossed the line, I was still into the whole experience, and enjoying how it felt to have done well. I was more or less only conscious of that. Breaking four minutes, I thought, would have been too good to be true. But then a friend of mine came running up to me and said that I had broken four minutes. But I didn't believe him. Or I should say, I wasn't going to let myself believe him. I knew that only the official time would count, so I didn't want to get my hopes up. But of course, the officials had me under four as well and I was absolutely amazed. I just couldn't believe it really. And the first thing I experienced was this tremendous, almost overwhelming sense of affirmation.

Affirmation of what?

Basically, that I was a respectable runner; that all the years I had put into training and racing, and all the sacrifices I had made finally paid off. It justified everything I had done in my track life up to that point. Which I suppose goes to show you that the 800's not the mile, and that 1:48's not 3:58. That race opened a whole new set of doors for me. In my own mind, breaking four gave me a key to this exclusive club that I had never imagined myself capable of entering, and that was just so thrilling. I had always had a reasonable belief in my ability, but to become a sub-four-minute miler . . . Wow, that elevated my opinion of myself as a runner to an entirely new level, and I felt just great about it . . . and I felt great about myself. And really, it's what has kept me training these last eight years, that race. Why else do you think I'm still carrying on running? Because I think I can do better; I want to have that sub-four experience again, and hopefully run even faster than 3:58.

That strikes me as really odd, Desmond, because I thought four minutes wasn't even an aspiration for you. Like you said, your entire mind-set was that of an 800 man, and to be honest, you weren't even supposed to be in that mile race, then suddenly it's like you're a new person?

Exactly, that's why I said it was an accident that I became a miler.

But it sounds almost transformational, that race, more like a born again experience than an accident?

Absolutely, it was transformational. That race was a life defining moment for me. Because I believed that if I could pull out such an established landmark in running, one I had grown up admiring, and something that was like a dream or an impossibility to me, and without the proper preparation, then I must possess a reasonable amount of ability or talent. And up to that point in my career, I was never certain about that. So immediately I redefined my identity, and my goals as a runner. I wasn't an 800-meter runner anymore. I was a miler.

# Exploring Boundaries

## MARKO KOERS
### (Netherlands)

First sub-4: January 20, 1996, 3:59.70, Champaign, Illinois
Personal best: 3:53.47
Total sub-4s: 3

*T*he *witness recounts a public event that transpired in full or partial view. He offers a perspective on the truth, one advanced from the outside looking in. And this testimony, this personal-experience story, should carry veracity, respect, and authority. Western culture is so visual. Description, explanation, knowledge . . . they all arise through seeing. But experiences are more than visual; they are also visceral. Movement, for example, is embodied and ephemeral. And sport combines blood, bones, and emotion to produce a result. The experience of a game isn't like the film shot or the picture painted . . . no permanent record remains. However fleeting it may be, though, skilled movement is still beautiful to behold; it has a soul, after all, and an essence that lies in the heart of the actor.*

*Of the countless mile races I have witnessed, few remain more vivid in my mind than Marko Koers's first sub-four-minute mile. He was a young Dutch runner over in America on a college athletic scholarship. I was a running enthusiast living in the same town. I befriended Marko and began to follow his progress, noting carefully his rises and falls. Perhaps as a witness I know more about his career than he does? And perhaps I can incite the sense of movement in him all over again.*

Marko, what does running mean to you?

Do you mean in terms of racing or my everyday training?

For example, as a professional runner what do you think about or consider when you're out running?

Maybe one important thing for me when I run is a sense of freedom.

Freedom to do what you want?

Or the freedom to learn new things, or go places, or understand nature. For example, in Florida where I sometimes base myself during the winter for warm-weather training, there is a forest where I can run among deer, snakes, turtles, and all kinds of birds. I love this about my running. Whenever possible I try to run in remote or natural areas.

What about the big cities across Europe that you travel to for your races?

Always when I get to a city, I ask at the front desk of the hotel where the nearest park or forest is. I'll do anything to avoid running on the street. One time when I was in Zurich, I got so carried away in this beautiful park running up and down different hills that I ran for an hour longer than I planned. But it was worth it. And luckily this was the day after my race so it didn't affect my performance.

Is running ever a form of escape for you?

No, I wouldn't say that. Although I can really lose myself in a run, and get carried away with the surroundings. For me, running is more about exploration. Exploring some new trail or different path. I think even when my hard competition days are over I'll continue to run because of this sense of exploration I have. It's very rewarding to me.

Will you miss the competitive aspect of running when your career is over?

Sure, the excitement of racing, improving, and traveling to races is a buzz. But the simple pleasures I experience running matter most.

Has running always had this feeling of freedom and exploration for you?

I used to run to school when I was a boy. And I got the biggest kick out of cutting through little bushes and green areas in my village, and hopping over bumps, or bounding up hills, or skipping around corners. And I'd do all of this as quickly as I could.

Were you trying to beat the school bus or something?

No, I just thought it was really boring to walk to school. I loved being outside. And around my village I explored every alley, road, or path. I knew every trail and hideout, and I was always looking for new ones. I had short-cuts to get from here to there; I might take a certain route and then duck off into the woods and dig up some dirt, or pick some berries, or build a hut.

Would you do this alone or with friends?

Sometimes by myself, but sometimes with another friend. Maybe it's best to think of me as an explorer-runner, someone who uses running to explore himself and his surroundings.

That sounds very philosophical.

Isn't running also philosophical? For sure it's psychological. Like how you have to learn to deal with tactics and pain, and of course winning and losing. Partly, I suppose I also enjoyed exploring my village as a boy because I had some natural stamina. For example, I could go running and walking and climbing for hours without even getting tired.

But that's to suggest that your inclination toward running was largely physical, whereas wouldn't you say that your interest in running was also due to certain mental characteristics you possessed? Like a disposition to enjoy the simple thrill of movement for its own sake?

That's right, because I wouldn't get bored traipsing around the forest for hours, whereas maybe a lot of other kids would have. They'd probably rather play games than go off alone looking here, there, and everywhere.

But good stamina comes in handy in games, too?

It does, and actually my natural enjoyment of running increased even more because of one schoolyard game we played called Fishnet. Basically, in this game you try to dodge everyone in the playground for as long as possible, and I was always the last person caught. And it gave me the most incredible rush to be good at something, and to do better than everyone else.

Did that feeling of success or achievement carry on once you began training and racing more formally?

In the first few organized races I ran, I found that I could beat people and win medals, and this felt great. Especially when I could pass older and bigger kids. I really liked doing that. But to be in front, or to differentiate myself from the others, that was always important for me. I guess that's natural, and something all children try to do.

Has there ever been a point in your running career when winning and getting recognition became more important to you than exploring or learning something new about yourself or your environment?

Oh, that's hard to answer. I don't know. But I think those two things have always been on an equal level with each other. Actually, if I have to be honest, I improved very slowly as a runner, so it wasn't this rush of immediate success that kept me involved. I think it was and has always been the pleasure, and then also the friends I began to make.

That kind of attitude must be difficult for you to maintain in today's world of professional running that is so much about winning, results, and rankings?

That's true. Sometimes it is hard for me to keep my focus and remember what I value about running. Especially when things aren't going well. If I'm injured, or I'm in a little bit of a slump . . . well, I can easily start to feel like a bum. That's also when people tend to put more pressure on me, which is exactly the wrong time to pressure a person, when he is feeling a bit low.

Do people ever ask you, "When are you going to get a real job?"

All the time. And occasionally I feel myself that I'm not living a proper or correct life as a responsible adult. But really, I cherish the time that I have. I feel blessed not to have to wake up early every morning and fight through traffic to get to work. I think I'm lucky that I can put true quality into my life. I can concentrate on doing this one thing very, very well—running faster times, and succeeding in championships like the Olympic Games. And when it all comes together, either in a race or following a good workout, that's extremely satisfying.

What is a typical workday like for you?

Well, basically I need to do two things every day: run in the morning, and run in the afternoon. In between I'll take a nap, eat, and probably stretch or get a massage. Whatever I need to do to stay rested and keep training at my best day after day.

I guess you can see why some people might consider that to be an easy life. But obviously there's a lot you're trying to manage and coordinate even though your routines are quite simple?

I don't really feel like I should have to defend why I lead my life the way I do. For now, running full time is what I enjoy, and I'll continue to do it as long as I feel it's a productive way to live.

Who are the people in your life that support you and your running?

Well, my parents, of course. And my coach, my agent, my sponsors, and the other runners I train with. I think it's the most important thing to be around people who think in a similar way. For example, with my training group we hardly ever talk about times and rankings. And my coach always says that I have to think about running relaxed. He doesn't want me to have to force anything. I need to get my technique down perfectly, he says. Because it's true, I live in this hyper world of time, competition, and prize money. And that can affect my decisions. For example, if I get too eager or impatient I might overtrain and possibly injure myself. But on the other hand, it's just a game I'm playing; I'm outside enjoying myself with good friends every day. I try always to remember that part.

As a boy, did you try other sports besides running?

Soccer naturally, because every boy in Holland tries soccer. But I didn't like it. I hated the contact, and as a young boy I don't think I was as coordinated as the others. But I'm not such a sporting person, anyway. I don't follow games and results in the newspaper or on television. Really, sport was not such a big deal in our family. My father sometimes watched soccer on Saturday night, but I never remember us having conversations at home about sport. School was always much more important. I was told to try my hardest at school and concentrate on that.

So what led you to come out of the forest, so to speak, and begin running competitively?

My older cousin was a runner. And in my mind, he was this very cool guy whom I admired and looked up to. One day at a family reunion he wasn't there and I wanted to know where he was. It turned out that he was at a track meet. So I thought, too, *Maybe I'll join a track club?*

And how old were you then?

Eight.

Is running a popular sport in Holland?

I wouldn't say so. It's not our main sport at least. For example, when I first joined my track club I didn't know about any legends or stories of famous Dutch runners from the past. The only runner I knew was my cousin. Then again, I don't think I'm such a legend type of guy, or someone who believes in them and gets inspired by them. If that was the case, I probably wouldn't have become a runner. I would have done cycling or something else that had more prestige and recognition in Holland. Even today I don't know too much about the history of running. It's not something I think about. Like who's who, or who did this and who did that. Back in school when we learned about the nautical mile and the land mile as different measuring systems around the world, I didn't know that the mile was also a track distance. Maybe it was after the movie *Chariots of Fire* that I began to realize some of the traditions of running. Well, the traditions in England at least. But when I did begin to learn more about the mile, and subsequently the 440 and 880, I thought it was so strange to have these odd distances that must have started and finished in different places on the track. You see, I was a little naive and didn't understand that the first tracks back in England and America were a quarter mile long, or 440 yards. I had assumed that all tracks everywhere in the world were 400 meters.

Do you know who Roger Bannister is?

No.

He was the first person to run under four minutes for a mile?

Ahhh, the four-minute mile, of course I know about that. But not until I went to university in America. In America everyone knows about the magic of four minutes. I have to say that to me that was truly amazing. In Holland a mile is never put on. I only heard about it being run in Oslo or the really big invitationals. Even then, in my mind, the mile was more of a race to do for fun. But I have to say that in America I got very excited about four minutes, and it became something I really wanted to do. And I wanted to do it not only for myself, but for others, too.

Like who?

I think if you want to become someone in running in America you better be a sub-four-minute miler. Before I broke four minutes, Americans couldn't really appreciate my running even though I had been to the Olympics and run 1:45 for 800 meters and 3:38 for 1500 meters. Sure, people knew I was a good runner, but breaking four minutes for the mile, I realized, would definitely increase their estimation of me and my ability. I think that's typical in America: A person's identity so often becomes a statistic that describes him, like being a sub-four-minute miler. I suppose that makes it easier to create legends, myths, and enormous amounts of hype. But in saying that, I have to admit that the magic of four minutes really infected me. And in my first mile race I was very determined to get below four minutes.

Did you think it would be hard to do?

Yes and no. I knew I could do it given my best 1500, and I calculated very carefully the splits I needed to run. But still I was nervous because of how much everyone wanted me to do it.

Yeah, I remember, there was a very big crowd that afternoon.

That's right. The new indoor track stadium had just opened on campus, and we were really trying to promote track and field and make it exciting.

Did the pre-race atmosphere jazz you up?

It was fantastic. Really, really exciting. Especially how the bleachers came right out to the edge of the track so the crowd was almost on top of you. And there was music playing, and the guys in the shotput and pole vault all stopped their events to watch.

You probably didn't realize it, but as you were warming up and completing your final strides everyone in the stands was watching you.

I didn't know that. I think I was pretty focused by that point.

What were you thinking about as you approached the starting line?

The same thing I always do when I run a mile or 1500 meters. How I needed to stay as relaxed as possible through the half, and then gradually increase the pace before gathering myself for a kick finish.

Did everything go as planned?

It did. The rabbit did a good job and brought me through halfway without any problems, and then I was out in front running just working and working.

Could you hear the crowd at all? Because everyone was screaming and cheering you on.

I remember the noise building and building every lap, particularly as I continued to stay on pace for four minutes—58, 1:59. It was such a surprise to me, even during the race, how important this four minutes really was. For example, I heard the public address announcer yell out my three-quarter mile time and say something like, "Koers is on target for four minutes, ladies and gentlemen." And I remember thinking, *Wow, this is something else. I better keep going.*

I think the crowd knew that you had committed yourself to getting under four, and they were right behind you.

That was what I sensed. And it made me feel responsible to a degree.

Responsible for what?

I suppose to entertain the audience and to honor their traditions and what they valued about track and field. Certainly it was a dramatic race for me, and a very special moment in my career.

Do you remember the scene when you crossed the line?

Oh, the house was going crazy. The electronic clock on the side of the track had stopped before four minutes, so everyone got what they wanted, including me. I don't think I'll ever forget my first taste of the magic of the four-minute mile.

Now that you are well under four minutes as a miler, do you have any new mile goals?

I'm not so happy with my 3:53 anymore. Now I need to run under 3:50. That to me is a good time. It's the new four-minute barrier, I think, and I want to break it.

Will that be hard for you to do?

It's hard in the sense that there are few opportunities to go for it. The European meetings don't often schedule a mile. That means I have to get it absolutely right on the day.

Why not go to America again? You have a good record there for that sort of thing.

That's a possibility. I'd love to do it there. I think in Eugene, Oregon they have a good mile race that goes under 3:50. But you know, because I have run 3:33 for 1500 meters, I should be able to run 3:49. Also, the races today are always so fast because of the Africans. I just need to get into a good race and hang on. That's the best way to run a new personal best . . . follow the Africans.

How is it to run against the Africans?

I suppose I have to think about it as a good thing, because with Africans in my race I have a better chance of improving my time. To be honest, when I run against the Africans I'm not even thinking about winning. I'm thinking, top 5 or top 10, and like I said, hopefully improving my time. That's my focus, improving my status by improving my time. I know that doesn't sound very heroic, but I feel that winning isn't an option for me these days, especially in a top race. That's the reality: it's so incredibly hard to win against the Africans.

So what's your strategy in a race with Africans?

To hang on. I have to get off the line quickly and into good position. The Africans always start fast and immediately form a straight line. It's the most important thing to be on this long train if you want a good time. Otherwise, you are wasting energy fighting for position at the back. To be honest, that's what my running is about today: trying to follow or stay close to the Africans and get a new PB [personal best]. It's got nothing to do with romantic tales of victory and glory and that sort of stuff.

So fast PBs determine everything?

Yes. Every year I need to run faster and faster times. It's the only way I'm going to survive as a professional runner.

Photo: AP / Wide World

# Smooth Miler

## NOAH NGENY
### (Kenya)

First sub-4: July 16, 1997, 3:50.41, Nice, France
Personal Best: 3:43.40
Total sub-4s: 13

*The body of an in-shape, in-form miler is sharp and specific. It's functional, like a well-designed instrument that's balanced and precise; it's hard but smooth like polished marble, and it's defined, direct, and exact like a cat's eye. So tuned is Noah Ngeny that he seems to occupy no space at all. By no means, though, is he small or inconsequential, even at just 140 pounds. The word* small *doesn't convey his boundless speed and strength. Would you call a bird that grazes past your head* small? *Movement as a sensation translates large.*

*Noah leads me up the stairs of his London house to the lounge. I listen to the sounds his bare feet make against the wooden steps. It's a pressing sound mixed with a tap followed by a tiny twist. Noah sits down cross-legged on a billowy chair. I sit opposite him on a firm couch as he begins to rub his feet in thick broad strokes.* Such fast feet, I think to myself. *Now his fingers are sliding between his toes. Those feet have covered a mile with amazing pace. He pushes his right thumb into his left arch. I try not to stare.*

*A runner's feet are where intention, effort, and force converge to deliver a result. The feet bear the heaviest burden of body weight and energy. They need to be resilient and tough. They need to be sleek, fast, and proud.*

Noah, can you tell me how you developed into a miler?

Well, to be honest, I didn't really do anything deliberate. It was an accident or just a lucky discovery that I am a miler. I was first an 800-meter runner. That was my event in Kenya and the race that I believed would be best for me. I never ran a mile until I came to England.

When was that?

In July 1997, I came to England for the first time. I wanted to be a runner at the highest level so I had to come to Europe. I arrived from Kenya on Friday and the next day, Saturday I went to run a mile race in Scotland. That was my first-ever race in Europe, and so also my first mile race. I didn't really know anything about the mile except that if I want to be a runner I have to race. So I'm okay about going to Scotland to run even if it's not an 800 and even if I am still very tired from my trip.

But you were familiar with the 1500 meters, right? Previously, had you run any 1500s before that first mile race?

Yes, once or twice, and I knew a mile is like the 1500, but I think it must be different, too.

What did you think would be different?

It is longer and so maybe I can't finish. And the start is not the same, or the marks on the track for split times.

So did you finish?

Oh, yes. It was all right.

What was your time in that race?

It was a 4:01.

That's a good result for your first time running a mile.

Thank you. But it was a strange race for me. And there is a story here. I really didn't know what I was supposed to be doing. I didn't know about pacing or how fast to come through for each lap. That was why I stayed in the middle with the other runners and waited. All I was told before the race was that the crowd wanted to see a sub-four-minute mile. But what does that mean? I wanted to ask someone but then I decided not to worry and just watch the other runners. I only learned later that the race was organized by a Scottish man who is trying to have a four-minute mile run in every Scottish village. So it was a small town we were running in, but the people were everywhere yelling and screaming for the first four-minute mile in their town. But I didn't know or understand.

What place did you get in that race?

I won.

You won. So then the people didn't get their four-minute mile.

They didn't and they weren't happy, especially the organizer man. And I felt bad for him.

But he couldn't have been mad at you. It was your first time running the mile. Did he even know who you were?

No, nobody was upset with me. Afterward the people were patting me on the shoulder and rubbing my head and giving me all kinds of congratulations and saying, *Good, good.* They were mad at the other runners from Britain in the race who were supposed to run hard and make sure the pace is good for four minutes, but they didn't. When we made halfway the time was, I think, around 2:01 and it felt very easy to me.

Did you take the lead at that point?

Yes, I took the lead and ran from the front then. Only I didn't understand to try to run faster against the clock because I was so close to breaking four minutes. I was running to win the race, that was all I really knew to do. I felt upset for the people because had I understood, I could have easily run that little bit faster for them. But after that day I understand the four-minute mile and that for English people it's important. At the same time it became important to me, too.

So you wanted another try at breaking four minutes?

Kim [McDonald], my coach, said right away that I should run the mile again. He told me that I looked easy and that I can definitely run faster, especially under four minutes. I trusted him and let him decide my next race. I knew Kim was probably right because that 4:01 was nothing for me. I was not tired at all.

And so a week later in Nice, in your second race ever in Europe, and your second time running the mile, you broke four minutes.

That was a very different day and race from the Scottish mile. Right from the start the pace was fast and I'm thinking, *Oh, we are running today.* My 800 split was 1:53, but like in Scotland still I'm not very tired so I decide to keep running hard.

And you ran 3:50, an 11-second improvement in one week and the fastest first sub-four-minute mile ever run. Was that a surprise to you?

I knew in Nice that I would break four minutes. There were so many good runners there. It was never a question for me.

Were you pleased?

Very much. Also in the week before that race I had been hearing stories about the four-minute mile and learning of the history of Roger Bannister and all the great men who ran the mile, even the Africans Filbert Bayi and Kip Keino. Before this time I didn't know so much about famous milers and I'm thinking maybe I can be all right at the mile. But first I know that I have to break four minutes.

Do you know that some milers try for years to run a sub-four-minute mile?

I do know this. I can see at meetings here in England when a runner breaks his first four-minute mile and he is very happy even if he is last place. I like that and think it is good. But for me it really came without trying, just running close to the front in Nice.

Did Nice make you forget about the 800?

Yes, I decided that I am a miler now. And I start thinking that I can run the mile faster.

Were you thinking that you could set a new mile world record?

No. I didn't know what the world record was. All I was thinking was, *Try and run faster.*

So breaking the mile world record was never a goal for you?

Not until my race with Hicham [El Guerrouj], in Rome in 1999, when he set a new mile world record and I finished second. Before that day I didn't think it was possible for me to set a record. Because even though I lost that race I also ran under the old record. That was when I think the record could be mine someday.

Which would make you the first Kenyan to hold the mile world record.

Yes, I know that, too. I would like to break the mile world record for Kenya.

What do you remember about that record race in Rome?

Oh, it was very hard.

Not like Scotland or Nice?

No, no, no. I was on the ground for a very long time afterward. I was tired and sick and uncomfortable. I don't think I was fit enough to run so fast that day.

How did you do it then?

Kim was just shouting to me from the side of the track to keep going and not let Hicham get too far ahead. Really, Hicham did the hard running and I was only trying to keep as close as I can.

What did you think when you heard your time?

At first I didn't believe it. It wasn't for five minutes after the race that I found out it was a new world record for Hicham. I was just on the ground so tired. But I was surprised with my time, even though I knew it was a fast race because I heard splits.

Do you have plans now to break the mile world record yourself?

I hope I can become fit enough. That is the most important thing, to train hard all through the year. If I become fit then maybe it is possible this season.

What kind of workouts are you doing now?

It's winter so I am just putting in many kilometers here in London through the parks and at home in Kenya through the country. Soon I go back to Kenya for more training because it's warm. I hate the cold and London is such a cold place.

You should try wearing socks. Are your feet cold?

Oh, no, they are okay. I just keep rubbing them.

# Miles of Time

## DAN WILSON
### (United States)

First sub-4: February 4, 2001, 3:59.14, Boston
Personal best: 3:59.14
Total sub-4s: 1

$Y$*outh, cynics say, is wasted on the young. All that exuberance, passion, and energy squandered on an innocent. Where's the justice in that, the middle-aged lament. After all, if experience is our wisest teacher, why give the young—the inexperienced, the naive—the greatest opportunity to change and prosper?*

*But life involves all of us in its changing times and impulses. There is a season to strive and compete, there is a season to reflect and settle. And clearly a miler's time exists in the former.*

*To charge ahead over a last-lap sprint, to sacrifice warmth for winter months of 100-mile weeks, and to dream of success, those are the qualities to admire in today's young miler. Talent, confidence, and ambition fuel his body; inhibitions fade as visions of speed and victory coalesce and converge. The young miler exudes beauty; he knows what lies inside him: the ease of movement, the rhythm of pace. And as his goals materialize or not, he will, like all milers before him, come to understand the futility of*

*regret, and the foolishness of cynicism. He will in the end acknowledge that the mile is*
*a young man's game.*

Dan, now that you've just graduated from college, do you have plans to continue running or is that it for you?

I'm definitely continuing. In fact, I've just moved to North Carolina to join a running group that has been created especially for postcollegians who want to keep training and pursuing their goals. And I'm finding the support really fantastic. It's a scheme called ZAP Fitness, set in the hills and forests of this small town, Blowing Rock; what an absolutely beautiful place to train. As part of the deal, all my expenses are covered, including health, and I receive a monthly living stipend. I have an apartment where I sleep, but everyone eats together in a large dining hall. So right now all I really have to worry about is running fast.

Sounds great. How many other runners are part of the program?

Eight at present, and everyone's American. ZAP's primary purpose is to raise the standard of American distance running. For example, we're all committed to making the next Olympic team in 2004. And not only making the team, but having an impact at the Olympics as well.

Who's funding all of this?

We're a not-for-profit organization so we rely on donations and gifts from sponsors. There are also money-making facilities on site, like a dormitory where track teams or running clubs can hold training camps. I have to say, in terms of pursuing my running, there is nowhere else in the United States I'd rather be right now. This is a great opportunity that I plan to take full advantage of.

So you're a professional runner now?

Well, let's say I'm a full-time runner. I've actually never made a single penny from running, but I do expect to one day. And I think living here in a quiet, focused place without any distractions is the best way for me to achieve my goals.

What are your goals?

To begin with, I'd like to have a long career and hopefully go to a couple of Olympics. Running in the Olympics, after all, is the highest honor for any runner, and I'd really like to experience that more than once. I'd also like to accumulate a number of sub-four-minute miles. When I look at guys like Steve Scott and Marcus O'Sullivan, who have run over 100 sub-fours, I think, *Wow, that's amazing.* I'd like to get to the point where every time I hop into a mile race I know I can get under four minutes. More immediately, though, it's crucial that I find a fast mile race in the coming year and improve my best time. I'm really expecting a big breakthrough in the mile next season. That's one of my most pressing concerns. I'm not worried, though, I know a fast time is inside me.

How do you know that?

I just do. There's no way I'm going to end my career with a personal best of only 3:59.

Tell me your idea of a big breakthrough in the mile.

Low 3:50s. Maybe 3:51 or 3:52. And that's not something I just hope will happen in the next year or two. At this point it's only a matter of when and where.

You're that confident?

I am.

Have you always believed so strongly in yourself?

I'd say so. For example, in high school I was sure I was going to be an elite runner someday even though my times weren't always the best around. I felt

I had a lot of growth and improvement in me, and that I was better than most other guys. I'm not sure how I came to believe that, though. Maybe it was some inner desire I possessed to be the best? I don't know. But in every race I ran, I always seemed to put myself in a position to win. I may not have ended up winning, but it was the feeling that I could have won that gave me confidence.

Have you established a time frame for yourself to reach your goals?

No. I'm willing to take all the time I need.

Do you think living somewhere isolated and secluded like Blowing Rock, North Carolina, is a necessary condition to succeed as a distance runner?

I think making sacrifices is important to become a successful distance runner. And I've given up a lot for this, like leaving my friends and family back home in Connecticut. And I do think having fancy cars and other stuff like that can distract you from your purpose. So, yes, living away from a busy nightlife, for example, does make it easier to remain focused. That's what's so good about this facility: I'm surrounded by other dedicated runners. And we strengthen and reinforce each other's commitment. I suppose I could've done what so many other runners do after college and gotten a job and tried to balance work with running, but I didn't want to do that. I wanted to make a 100 percent commitment. It's the right time in my life to give running a shot, and I'll never have as good an opportunity as this again.

What do your parents think of what you're doing?

They're very supportive. They always have been. In college they came to all of my meets. My dad's continually telling me, "You can get a job at any time in life." He wants me to do this now. "Run while you're still young," he says to me.

Have you changed your training in any way to reflect your new professional commitment to running?

I know that I have to work harder now than I ever have before, there's absolutely no way around that. Much of my previous success, I have to admit, came quite easily. But to move up to the next level, to reach world class, I have to put in more miles for a start. In college I normally ran 70 miles a week, whereas now I'm running 90. I also used to run small 5K road races now and then, but I won't be doing that anymore. I'm not letting anything that's not part of my bigger plan distract me. After all, if America is going to get back on top in track more postcollegians have to stick with the sport. Also, more groups for postcollegians like ZAP need to form so guys have the support to continue running. That was what American runners did back in the 1970s—they trained single-mindedly in places like Florida and Eugene, Oregon—and honestly, that's the only way we'll ever be good again.

What do you think the current problem is with American distance running?

We're just getting totally destroyed on the world level. Partly, I think it's because we don't train hard enough, at least compared to the Kenyans and Moroccans. There are also so many other sports that kids here can choose to do. And there's practically no money or attention in track so our best athletes go out for other sports—and who can blame them, really? In some ways it's a numbers game: We don't get many kids choosing to be distance runners, whereas the African countries get loads. That limits our selection base, thus giving us a fraction of the depth. As a Kenyan, being a good runner is considered very prestigious, and an excellent way to make a living. One winner's check from a road race in Europe or the States can support an entire family for a year. But that's not the case here. So of course more guys from there than from here are going to try to be world-class runners. It's much easier, after all, to support yourself with a regular job. Not many people want to run 90 miles a week year in and year out when they don't have to. Being a distance runner is hard. Much harder than some cushy office job.

But you want to try to make a living that way—why?

Running's in me, I think. I love it. I don't know, it just feels like something I have to do. In some ways, I guess, it is me: I am a runner.

Do you think there is any way to make track a more appealing sport to U.S. kids and as a result increase the running population?

Well, one thing that seems to be helping is this whole Alan Webb phenomenon. A couple of years ago when he became the first high school runner since 1967 to break four minutes for the mile, that really rejuvenated interest in the sport. Which is great because he's creating a future fan base. And a recognizable star is what we need to boost people's interest in running. You only have to look at Tiger Woods's effect on the popularity of golf to know that. In fact, most people who find out I'm a runner ask me right away if I've raced against Alan Webb. It's incredible. The only other question anyone asks me is if I've broken four minutes for the mile. I also think the U.S. collegiate system may not be the best way to develop young talent. We have to race hard three seasons in a row: cross-country, indoors, and outdoors. Maybe if we took a season off every year to train and build ourselves up, that would be better. That's what the top Kenyans do. They focus on one season, the summer in Europe, and the rest of the year they train. And just look at the results they get. They're unbeatable. So maybe it's about time we began learning from them?

Would you say your motives to succeed as a runner are patriotic, or more internal and self-directed?

Maybe a bit of both. I'd like to see U.S. runners get more respect, not only at home but on the international circuit as well. So anything I could do in that regard would be great. But my goals are very personal, too, and achieving them is really important to me.

Given the present running climate in America, do you think an American will ever hold the mile world record again?

Oh, that's a tough one. I don't want to sound like the bearer of bad news but the way it's looking . . . well, I don't know. It's hard to imagine that happening right now. We're definitely in a rut, and it doesn't look like that's about to change anytime soon. Something drastic needs to happen for us to catch up with the Africans. Most of the young American runners I know aren't even talking about beating the Africans. And that won't change until someone comes along and shows that it's possible for a U.S. distance runner to compete with the world's best.

Could that someone be you?

I hope so.

Do you ever feel, Dan, that the way you're pursuing your running goals with such determination and commitment is some type of romantic quest or journey that you're on?

Actually, a lot of my friends think what I'm doing is really cool. Although I'm not sure they'd do something similar. You know, live out a dream at the expense of career and all that stuff. But I've always had goals and ambitions as a runner. Like breaking four minutes. That was definitely a dream of mine.

How did your idea of a four-minute mile as a great achievement arise?

After I read *Once a Runner*, by John Parker, in my sophomore year of high school, Quentin Cassidy, the main character who is trying to break four minutes, became my hero. I really identified with him, what he wanted, and how he led his life. So sub-four became important to me, because I wanted to be like Quentin. But it took a while before I really believed it was possible. At first I thought a four-minute mile was this unbelievable achievement, like the ultimate performance in a runner's life. And there were some local college runners I knew when I was in high school who had run 4:05 and I thought they were gods. But as I progressed and my times dropped, my thoughts slowly changed. Then in my senior year of high school I ran 4:15 and my coach told me that I could definitely break four one day. I suppose I didn't quite believe him at first, but at least it was something I was beginning to see.

How did your mile time progress beyond high school?

My freshman year of college, 1998, I improved to 4:08. But during the course of that year I beat a few guys who had run 4:02. Because of that my confidence really grew. Then two years later, in the spring of my junior year, things changed dramatically. I ran a 1500 in 3:39, which was an improvement of about five seconds. And do you know what I said to my coach almost immediately after finishing that race? I said, "I have to find a mile race." Because I knew that 3:39 was roughly the equivalent of a 3:56 mile, and my best mile time at that point was only 4:05, and I was absolutely desperate to get under four minutes.

That is an interesting reaction given that it's more important to have a fast 1500-meter time under your belt than a sub-four-minute mile if you want to qualify for the major international championships.

I know, but it was just this huge coming-of-age barrier that I desperately wanted to achieve. My coach felt the same way, in fact. And so did my dad. It was the first thing he said to me after that race: "Dan, we've gotta find you a mile to run."

And did you?

Well, that's the sad thing with running in the U.S. The good meets dry up once the collegiate season ends. But I did find a race in Homedale, New Jersey. It didn't work out, though. The field was pretty weak, and it was a cold and rainy day. I won by five seconds and ran 4:00.7.

Oh, so close. That must have been frustrating?

No, not really, because I was pretty sure at this point that I'd get it the next time I tried. And I did.

That was in Boston, right, indoors at Harvard?

Yeah, and my only goal in that race, I have to say, was to break four minutes. I didn't even care that much what place I got; if I ran under four, that was good enough for me.

Had you specifically targeted that meet as your next best opportunity at breaking four?

Actually, that race kind of came together at the last minute. I was planning to train through the indoor season that year in order to concentrate on outdoors. But when I heard about this race at Harvard with a stacked mile field I thought maybe I should jump into it. I asked my coach what he thought and he agreed. So right away we changed all of my workouts for the next few weeks and I did a series of special sessions just to get ready to try to break four minutes that day. So all of a sudden, there I was in January doing workouts I wasn't planning to do until May. But that made it exciting, too. Like there was this really special event we were going all out to prepare for.

Would you have changed your training program so abruptly to run in a stacked 1500-meter race?

No. I only did it because I wanted to break four minutes for the mile. That was the only reason.

So you had a lot riding on that race.

It didn't seem like that, really. Although my parents did come to watch me, and a bunch of my college friends had driven up to Boston to cheer me on, too.

Did having your friends and family focusing on this one race and this one time, sub-four, create a lot of extra pressure for you?

I think the excitement and drama of four minutes, and the question, *Would I or wouldn't I break it*, made the whole day that much more fun. I knew what I could do; I was in great shape; I knew I could get under four. What's interesting, though, is that I could have been going for the world record at 1500 meters, but none of my friends would have driven three hours to see that. People are just so intrigued with the mile, particularly a sub-four-minute mile. It's amazing, really. Which is why it's strange that more meets don't hold miles, at least in the U.S. Because the mile is the one event that people can identify with. After all, who hasn't run or walked a mile at some point in their life?

What specifics do you remember about the race?

The pace wasn't that fast, I remember that. We were maybe 59 seconds at the quarter, then 1:59 at the half, and 2:59 at three-quarters. The arena was really loud, though—I definitely remember that. All the indoor meets at Harvard usually sell out. They do a great job promoting them, especially when they schedule a mile and pump up the whole sub-four thing.

Could you hear your family and friends cheering for you?

Not them, specifically. I could only hear this general roar of the crowd, which really psyched me up. I always try to use crowd noise to my advantage. I find it really gets my adrenaline going. Also, throughout the whole race the track announcer was screaming out splits to the crowd. And every time we reached the next quarter-mile mark on four-minute pace he'd yell out our time and the crowd would go nuts. I think they wanted to see a four-minute mile as much as we wanted to run one.

Were you running up near the front or hanging off the back?

I was in second or third, for the most part. And I remember feeling really comfortable there. Too comfortable, in fact, because coming into three-quarters I had this brief mental lapse and a couple of guys shot by me. But I quickly snapped out of it and started closing in on them really hard. There was less than a quarter mile to go at this point, and I knew I was still on pace to break four minutes because I had just heard the three-quarters time. But you never know what can happen over that last quarter mile, so it was a matter of putting my head down and digging as deep as I could. And basically, that was what I did. In the end, I just missed out on third. And immediately after I crossed the line I was looking around everywhere to try to find out my time and whether I had broken four.

You didn't have an immediate sense that you had done it?

Not at all. My dad, though, came running over to tell me that I had, but I wasn't going to trust his hand time, especially because he wasn't right next to the finish line. So I kept saying to him, *Just wait, Dad, just wait for the official time.* Because the worst thing that can happen is that you get all excited about some time you think you've just run only to find out a couple of minutes later from the officials that you've actually run a few tenths slower. And I knew it was going to be that close, so I didn't want to get my hopes up. Then finally an official came up to me with the good news. He was holding a photo of the finish with my result, 3:59.14. And right away I looked up at my family and friends in the stands and gave them the thumbs-up sign and they broke out into this huge cheer. It was a great moment. I mean, absolutely great. And straightaway I felt the most incredible high throughout my entire body. And it stayed with me for the next hour or so. When I went outside for my cool-down I actually felt as if I was running on air, and that I could go on running forever. It was like I couldn't make myself tired. I was going all around these different streets and neighborhoods in Boston, and up the Charles River, and the whole time feeling like nothing could stop me or slow me down. It was a fantastic sensation. Like my life was absolutely perfect and I had an endless source of energy. That continued when I arrived back into the arena and began running laps around the track. The meet had ended by this point and I pretty much had the track to myself. One of my teammates who had also run a good race that day joined me and together we were just cranking out lap after lap and all the while laughing and talking. We were just on top of the world.

Now that you've broken four minutes, do you think that it is somehow crucial in legitimizing your ongoing commitment to running either to yourself or to others?

I think every middle-distance and distance runner thinks about running sub-four. And sure, having done it might possibly legitimize my current lifestyle to nonrunners. But like I said before, I've always believed in myself, and that I had the ability to be a world-class runner, even way before I broke four minutes. Of course, breaking four has reinforced that, and definitely it was an important standard to achieve. But more important, I think, is my deep desire to be the best possible runner I can. And so more than anything else, that's why I'm still at it today.

Photo: Empics

# Time Traveler

## MIKE EAST
### (United Kingdom)

**First sub-4:** July 22, 2001, 3:59.61, London
**Personal best:** 3:59.61
**Total sub-4s:** 2

*Who says a four-minute mile isn't contemporary? Just look at what else survives from 1954, the year Roger Bannister ran the first sub-four. Won't we always be reading Hemingway? He won the Nobel Prize for Literature in 1954.* White Christmas *was number one at the box office that year, and* I Love Lucy *topped the television ratings. Both remain cultural icons today.*

*Yes, times have changed since Bannister's 3:59.4. After all, that was two generations ago. Britain, for instance, has more than one television channel today, and the average weekly wage in the United States has risen well above $75.30. But 10.2, 20.6, 45.8, 1:46.6, 13:51.2, and 28:54.2—all world records back in 1954—are still highly respectable times. Those marks aren't destined for a museum, and there's certainly nothing dusty or faded about the names of the men who set them: Stanfield . . . Rhodes . . . Kuts . . . Zatopeck. You can put Bannister in the same category: an enduring track-and-field icon.*

*The anthropologist Edward Said thinks museums are sad places because they rele-gate objects to artifacts and experiences to memories. "Museums freeze images in time," he said. "They deny them a spirit to change." So thank heaven that 3:59 survives out-side anyone's private collection, even Bannister's. It's a standard and an achievement that's alive and well today. And I've traveled to Plymouth, on England's southeast coast, to meet a 21st-century miler and find out why.*

Mike, as a young English middle-distance runner, and with that great tra-dition of mile world-record holders behind you—Wooderson, Bannister, Ibbotson, Coe, Ovett, Cram—do you dream of setting the mile world record yourself one day?

Not really. But the 1500 meter world record, it would be amazing to hold that. The 1500 just carries so much more currency than the mile. To be hon-est, a fast 1500 time would advance my career more than anything else. Running in the low 3:30s, for example, would get me into better races, secure me government funding, and improve my chances of attracting a sponsor. There's just so much more scope with a fast 1500 time besides your name as opposed to a fast mile, or for that matter a championship medal. That's what I think, anyway. It's also what my agent tells me: "Improve your 1500 time, Mike." And because I've recently quit my job to train full time, I have to think about the economics of running, and how to make a living.

But surely a fast mile time, or even better, the mile world record, would increase your marketability?

Maybe, but from everything I've seen from our governing body, UK Athletics, the mile doesn't seem to figure in any of their funding plans. It's just the 1500. In fact, last year one of the boys was going for a fast mile in London, but the officials had to set up a timer at 1500 meters so the British selectors could decide whether to send him to the World Championships. It didn't seem to make a difference what his mile time was. That right there tells you something about the mile's current status.

So is the mile an irrelevant distance today?

Somewhat, I think. Or maybe it's best to think of it as an exhibition event. Put it this way: I'd gladly run a mile if I had to, but given a choice I'd much rather run a 1500. If I ran a mile in 3:52, for example, I'd be upset knowing that with the same effort I could have ended up with a 3:34 1500, which as I said before would go a lot farther in advancing my career than a 3:52 would.

But what about your neighbor, or the average British sports fan—surely he'd be more impressed with a 3:52 mile than a 3:34 1500, or even a 3:25 for that matter?

He would, you're right, and that would be nice. But he's not funding me, is he?

Not directly, but by watching you run on television or buying a ticket to see you race he is. And isn't it important to cultivate the average sports fan's support, even if that means running miles over 1500s?

I see your point. But right now the future's in the 1500, and I need to concentrate on that.

Do you think your attitude toward the mile as an antiquated event is representative of your generation?

I do. As a teenager hanging around the track, back when I first started to run, the older guys used to go on and on about the mile. They thought breaking four minutes was a real indication of a runner's talent. My grandfather used to talk to me about the mile, too, and he'd say how fantastic it would be if I could break four minutes. But I don't know, maybe I was just an ignorant kid or something, but those old stories about the mile never impressed me that much. I even remember running a race up at Oxford—you know, on the track where Roger Bannister broke the four-minute mile for the first time—and all the old guys in our club were discussing the significance of that moment in British athletics. And I was like, *Yeah, all right.* I think I just saw my event as the 1500, not the mile. Primarily because I was running the 1500 week in and week out, not the mile. So they became two different events for me. I hardly ever remember running the mile as a lad. It

just wasn't part of any fixtures. And today when I'm down at the track training, kids always ask me what they need to do to improve their 1500 time.
Because for them, like me, the 1500 is the relevant standard for promotion
and advancement, not the mile.

Can I ask you about your training, then, and the rhythms in your head
when you're doing a track workout? Are you more oriented toward doing
intervals that are fractions of a mile, like 400s and 800s, or intervals that are
fractions of 1500 meters like 500s or 1000s?

Yeah, that's a bit of a contradiction, I suppose. Because all the intervals I
run on the track are based on the British Imperial System; like you said, 400s
which are obviously equivalent to quarter miles, and 800s which are equivalent to half miles. Even if I have to run 500s or 1000s I break that down to
a 400 plus a 100, or an 800 plus a 200.

You don't see a 300 or a 600, for example, as a "real" distance in itself?

No. I always make it a fraction of a 400, or in other words, a quarter mile.
All my pacing and pace judgment work, too, is done in terms of 400s. And
in a 1500 meter race, it's my 400 splits I'm listening to, nothing else.

So maybe the mile and its traditions are more embedded in your mind
than you think?

I wouldn't be surprised. I mean as a kid, Sebastian Coe and Steve Ovett
were massive idols of mine. I followed all their races, and read all their books.
And probably what I knew most about them was that they were the mile
world-record holders. I think if an English runner today could break 3:50
that would rejuvenate interest in the mile, particularly for kids. As it is now,
though, we're trying to catch up with the rest of the world's top middle-distance runners, and in order for us to do that we have to race them over the
1500. It's not enough to have a bunch of guys in England around four minutes or just under. To raise the mile's profile, we need someone who can compete with the world's best, which means running 3:48 at least. But you know,
I think it also requires a degree of luxury to be chasing a fast mile time. Look

at Coe and Ovett, and later Steve Cram. It really wasn't until they were established as the best middle-distance runners in the world that they began to attempt the mile world record. It's the same with Hicham El Guerrouj today, or Noah Ngeny. Those guys look to run the mile because it's a way for them to further their career by breaking another world record.

So the mile is secure as an event for the future?

Guys are always going to want to run a mile. It's so historic, and that will never go away. But in saying that, I still think that setting the 1500-meter world record will be the priority in most guys' minds.

It's interesting, Mike, but everything we've talked about thus far makes it seem as if running fast times is so much more important than winning races. How do you feel about that?

I know lots of people believe the problem with athletics is the extreme focus on times and records. They consider runners today to be a bunch of glorified time trialists. But there are always going to be some people who like to see fast times, and other people who like to watch competitive races. Personally, I prefer competitive races. I enjoy mixing it up in a tight pack and trying to figure out the best way to win. Those races where everyone runs around the track in single file can be really boring. And they do seem to be the norm these days, that's true. So in that case, I can see why some people are complaining.

Do runners today train as hard as runners from the past?

Well, the guys I run against week after week are all pretty hungry, and they're all training their hardest.

But what about the stories of guys back in the 1970s, like Dave Bedford, who used to run 200 miles a week?

I don't know if I could physically run 200 miles a week. As it is, I can hardly manage 75. I get so bored on runs longer than an hour, and I start to get hungry, too. I also need more in my life than just running. Putting in 200 miles a week wouldn't leave much time to do anything else. Then again, if I add up all the time I spend getting massages, having blood tests, getting my gait analyzed, or seeing sport psychologists, it probably takes as much time as running 200 miles a week.

That's an interesting point. The modern athlete's commitment is probably as great as guys from previous generations—it's just how you spend your time that's different.

I think we do more "smart training" than they did in the past. It's not only about putting in high mileage, after all. There are other things I can do to improve, like stretching or strength training or analyzing my diet. Training's become very scientific today. And being an athlete is definitely a full-time occupation. I swear there are days when I'm running around like a headless chicken.

Do you ever imagine yourself as this precise mechanical runner trying to be as exact and scientific as possible with everything you do?

In a way, that's the goal of my training: to learn as accurately as possible—for example, what 58 pace for 400 meters feels like versus 56 pace. I have to know that difference, otherwise I can't stick to my training schedules, or I might go out too fast in a race and then it's *game over.*

How do you learn that difference?

It's a timing thing, really. I run laps at varying speeds and try to internalize the qualities of a 58 lap compared to a 56 lap. It's a "feel" thing more than anything else. I'm not sure how to describe it, except to say that the sensation of moving at different speeds eventually gets fixed into my head and my legs. It's something I'm always working on: trying to absorb the perfect rhythm inside my body so I can run exactly as I want to.

Have you always run with a mind toward precision and efficiency?

No. For years I never used to think about what I was doing. I'd just throw on my trainers and head out the door. That worked for a while, until I stopped improving, and I knew I had to make a change. So last year I switched coaches. My old coach wasn't that analytical, and if I wanted to improve I knew I needed to work with someone who was.

What do you and your new coach discuss about your training?

Everything, really. We time and record all my runs; I use a heart-rate monitor; we're constantly measuring changes to my fitness, and how I'm responding to different workouts.

What workouts do you find the hardest?

I suppose the really intense, high-lactate speed sessions on the track. Because I know when I'm warming up for those sessions that they're going to be really painful. And that always makes me stop and think.

What do you think about?

I guess how badly I want to be a great runner, and that hard workouts come with the territory, so I just have to get through them.

Can you remember the first track workout you ever did?

Oh, yes, very clearly. It was a winter day and it was lashing down with rain. My dad took me to the track here in Portsmouth so I could run with the local club. This was after a schoolteacher had recommended to my father that I try athletics.

And how did it go?

I loved it, every last second, especially the rain.

Really, why?

I don't know, but somehow I could feel right away that this was something I was good at. I was up with the lead group running with a whole bunch of guys and I wasn't struggling at all. And afterward people were telling me I had done really well, including my dad. And because I never took my schooling that seriously, running became something that I could see myself succeeding at. So I went back the next week to another practice, and then again the next week. And that was it really, I had become a runner.

Do you still enjoy running in the rain?

I have to say that I hate it when the ground is soaked and muddy, or when the track is flooded. Right away, I can feel my muscles tightening as the water splashes on my legs. And when I need to hit times and turn out good results in training, rainy conditions make that hard.

What about running on the beach—do you take advantage of that, seeing as you live here on the southeast coast of England?

I don't like to run on the beach, either. If I was in Spain running over a smooth sandy surface that'd be different, but here there are so many pebbles and rocks on the beach that it's just bloody hard work. Also, because I'm tall and skinny the wind knocks me about. That's why I do all my long runs on the road, and around buildings, too: to try and get some shelter from the wind.

Is it still important for you to train with a group?

Yes, that's still very important to me. I enjoy the social aspects of belonging to a running club. It kills the boredom, and the support makes it easier to push through a tough speed session, or to kick at the end of a hard race. In fact, last year I ran the Emsley Carr Mile in London and when I walked onto the track from the holding area beneath the stands all my mates screamed, "Come on, Easty, you can do it." And I remember thinking to myself, *Those nutters.* But at the same time, it was great having them there.

That's the race where you broke four minutes for the first time, isn't it?

Yeah, that's the one. I knew you'd want to talk about that.

You're right, I do. So what can you tell me about it?

Well, it was at the Crystal Palace in London, there were 16,000 people in the stands, an international television audience, and Hicham El Guerrouj, the mile world record holder from Morocco, was shooting for a new world record.

Big stuff, then?

Huge. Absolutely huge. I practically lost me breath when I stepped onto the track and saw the crowd. There was just row after row of people. And in the holding area I was staring at El Guerrouj thinking, *My God, there's El Guerrouj.* I was just used to seeing him on telly; I even considered asking him for his autograph.

How did you get an invitation to such a big race?

I was actually having a pretty good season that year. I had run 3:38 for 1500 meters, and the week before I had placed fourth in the British championships. And at these British Grand Prix meets they always need some locals. So when they asked me if I wanted to run, of course I said yes, even though it was the end of my season and my legs were pretty used up. Not only that, the next week I was getting married and I was pretty occupied with wedding plans and other stuff. So really, I wasn't very focused going into that race.

You weren't thinking that it would be a great opportunity to get under four minutes for the first time?

That's what I should've been thinking, you're right. But honestly, I was more concerned with not embarrassing myself in front of such a huge crowd. Especially when I heard that El Guerrouj wanted a world-record pace, which was just so fast that I knew there was no way I was going to be up near the front. I also had a very defeatist attitude about breaking four minutes for some reason. I imagined it was something remarkable that only a few guys did. Which was strange because I had run some decent 1500s, and I knew that I only had to hang on for another 100 meters to crack four minutes. Yet I was still psyched out somehow. Maybe it had to do with all the history, or the older guys around the track when I was a kid who made four minutes sound superhuman. I don't know. But it was definitely a barrier in my mind when it shouldn't have been. Whether I was going to do it in that Emsley Carr Mile, though, was another story. I just wasn't geared up for that race at all. And it showed. By the second lap I was dead last.

What was your half-mile split?

Two minutes flat.

That's perfect.

I know. I know.

So didn't that encourage you?

I was surprised, to be honest. I thought I was running much slower because I was getting beaten so badly. But it did wake me up, and for the first time I thought, *All right, this isn't going so badly.* But then the pace picked up and immediately I fell farther back. I really felt awful, really bad, and just completely tired, drained, and wiped out. I felt so lonely, too, out there by myself at the back of the pack. It was as if everybody in the stadium was watching me and seeing what a loser I was, which of course they weren't, but that was how it felt.

Did you hear a time at three-quarters?

I didn't. But by that point I was just running to finish and end my misery as quickly as possible. I remember when I crossed the line I was so upset at coming last in this big race that I just wanted to hide from everyone. I thought maybe I had run 4:02 and then I heard some people say I was right around four minutes. But I didn't care. I didn't even want to see the results. I just wanted to go home. Then the official result came out, which was 3:59, and I was like, *Oh, wow, that's excellent.*

Really, your mood changed that quickly?

It did. Instantly. But I also had these massively mixed emotions. Okay, I had just broken four minutes for the first time, which felt fantastic. But I also came last. So should I feel elated or depressed?

And which way did you swing?

I decided to be pleased. It was my last race of the season, after all, and I was about to get married and go off on my honeymoon, so why not see it as a positive end to the year, to have broken through this historic barrier? In fact, I ended up getting the result sheet with my name and time on it framed. It's right there, on the wall in the lounge.

I bet your friends and family were pleased?

*Overjoyed* is more like it. No one seemed to care at all that I had come last, which is so interesting. They were just excited that I had broken four minutes . . . even more than me. It goes to show, I suppose, what four minutes means to people.

Now with four minutes under your belt, what would you like to achieve in your next mile race?

Instead of telling you some time I'd like to run, if I was to get the opportunity to run another mile I'd want to be more competitive. Especially now that my approach to running has become more professional. I literally can't afford to go into races anymore thinking I'm only there to fill out the field.

So given another opportunity to run against El Guerrouj, you wouldn't be starstruck?

Absolutely not. I'd be all business.

And do you see yourself sticking with the 1500/mile as your main event, or are you contemplating a move up to 5000 meters?

No, I think I'm best suited to the 1500. Besides, it's so much more prestigious than the 5K or any other event.

What makes you say that?

Well, the crowds come out for it, don't they? The 1500 gets the most attention of any distance event.

Now, I'd say that's because effectively the 1500 is tied to the mile and the prestige and history of four minutes.

Yeah, in some way I suppose you might be right.

And now that you're a sub-four-minute miler you're part of that history, too.

That's true. I guess I am.

# Epilogue

In an episode of *Batman and Robin* I saw as a boy, the Dynamic Duo were stranded by the side of the road exactly one mile from an impending crime scene. Desperate to foil the proceedings, they took to their feet and incredibly ran a three-minute mile. Shortly thereafter, when another emergency arose a mile away, our heroes produced a two-minute mile. I watched this, of course, in complete amazement.

Farfetched? Impossible? Perhaps, but who knows where the mile world record will fall one day? Clearly our Caped Crusaders had a number of superpowers at their disposal—remember those utility belts—but as sport becomes increasingly modernized and scientized with genetic modification, oxygen houses, and hormone replacements, aren't all athletes to some extent becoming superpowered? This is not the place, however, to discuss the evolving nature of competition and the ethics of fair play. The portraits in this volume, after all, have been less about winning and ambition than about turning point experiences and how individuals create their identity.

Despite obvious first appearances, running isn't strictly about finishing times and crossing the line first. Aren't friendships made, lessons learned, and rich and varied experiences had? Moreover, there's the joy of movement and how our bodies become instruments of beauty and pride. Specifically, a four-minute mile, it has to be said, is as much a highly prestigious public achievement as it is a highly private personal accomplishment. And as I have discovered in my lengthy conversations with the men in this book, understanding what it means to run four laps in four minutes involves far more than an explanation of the biomechanics of speed and the physiology of endurance.

Our athletic experiences can never be reduced to an impulse, or an equation, or a predictable chain of scientific events. A runner's life contains drama, expression, and surprise as stride by stride he thinks and reflects on who he is and why he runs; running involves power and courage—we heat up, our lungs and muscles press, and win or lose our lives expand. And yes, everyone in this book has immortalized the four-minute mile and mentioned its historical significance, but equally they have confirmed through their singular tales of triumph and transformation the unique pleasures of running and the everlasting satisfaction of achievement. And could a better testimony to the vitality of the four-minute mile exist than to see how 21 men from nine different countries over the course of 50 years have grown and prospered through its magic?

Roger Bannister may be the four-minute mile's poster child, but as the stories contained here attest, the four-minute mile's significance and importance clearly transcends his contribution. In the same way that Everest still summons climbers, so to do the rewards of running a four-minute mile beckon today's runner. It's the talk at any track where young runners congregate and speculate on their progress: *Could I run a sub-four-minute mile someday?* There are also the thousands of milers who approached the peak of their calling only to come up seconds short, running a 4:01 mile or thereabouts. And we know from their desperate testimonies of heartache and loss that they remain disappointed long into retirement. Such is the case with any highly sought-after and recognized standard of achievement like a four-minute mile: Some will reach the other side, some won't.

The future of the four-minute mile, therefore, seems secure. Yet, we must continue to do all that we can to guard its stature. Running is metric today, and more than anything else middle-distance runners advance their careers by posting superior metric marks. But room must still be made for the mile. It's the mile that truly challenges a runner's limits; it's the mile that captures the public's attention. One strategy to preserve the mile could be to allow individuals to qualify for major 1500 meter championships with an equivalent mile time. This might entice meet promoters, particularly in the United States and England, to include the mile on their program, thus protecting it from becoming an odd curiosity that's only contested occasionally. Favoritism? Special treatment? Maybe, but after all, shouldn't special steps always be taken to protect a world treasure?

# Appendix

## Biographies

**Jama Aden**, the former Somalian mile record holder, lives with his wife and three children in Sheffield, England. He is the national running coach and junior development coordinator of track and field for Sudan.

**Don Bowden** is founder and CEO of Tech-Tone, specialists in indoor and outdoor court surfaces. The former American-record holder in the mile lives in Saratoga, California, and is active in fostering young kids' interest in running.

**Sebastian Coe**, twice Olympic 1500-meter champion (1980, 1984) and past mile world-record holder, is the president of the English Amateur Athletic Association. He is the author of five books and an experienced broadcaster and public speaker.

**Steve Cram** is the 1983 1500-meter world champion, the 1984 Olympic 1500-meter silver medalist, and a former mile world-record holder. He keeps busy today as the BBCs track-and-field commentator, and the chairman of the English Institute of Sport. He lives with his wife and two children in the Northeast of England.

**Eamonn Coghlan** lives with his family in Dublin where he is the director of fund-raising and marketing for the Dublin Children's Hospital. He is the former indoor world-record holder for the mile, and 1983 world champion over 5000 meters.

**John Davies**, the Olympic 1500 meter bronze medalist in 1964, is a coach, athletics events organizer, and president of the New Zealand Olympic Committee. He is involved with numerous programs and events to promote sport in New Zealand as a positive and healthy experience.

**Mike East** is a full-time runner who lives in Portsmouth, England, with his wife of two years. He is the 2002 Commonwealth Games champion at 1500 meters, and is coached by 1988 Olympic steeplechase bronze medalist for Britain, Mark Rowland.

**Herb Elliott** remains one of Australia's legendary sports heroes. He is a former mile world-record holder and 1500 meters Olympic champion (1960). He generously involves himself in various public causes and issues related to sport. He currently lives in Melbourne, Australia.

**Desmond English** works in mergers and acquisitions for HSBC Bank in London. He is coached by Mike Barnow of Westchester Track Club (New York) and Warren Roe of Havering Mayesbrooke A.C. (London). Besides running he enjoys hiking and traveling.

**Martin Hemsley** resides in New York with his wife, Adrienne, and their four children Elizabeth, Matthew, Anne, and William. He is an options trader in New York City, an active runner, and a youth soccer and baseball coach.

**Derek Ibbotson** is past European representatve of the Puma Shoe Company. The former mile world-record holder enjoys travel and golf, and lives comfortably in his home county in Yorkshire, England.

**Marko Koers** is in the full swing of his athletic career following a sixth place finish in the 1996 Atlanta Olympics 1500-meter final. The Dutch national record holder for the mile lives and trains in Nijmegen, The Netherlands.

**John Landy** is the governor of the state of Victoria, Australia. In addition to being the former mile world record holder and Olympic bronze medalist over 1500 meters in 1956, he was recently inducted into the Scholar-Athlete Hall of Fame, where his contributions to the field of entomology were recognized.

**Noah Ngeny**, the Olympic 1500 meter gold medalist from the Sydney Olympics in 2000, is also the Kenyan national record holder for the mile. He trains as a full-time middle-distance runner between his homes in Kenya and London, and remains a dominant force on the world athletics scene.

**Jim Ryun** is a third-term U.S. Congressman from the Second District of Kansas. He won an Olympic silver medal in the 1500 meters in 1968, and he is the last American to hold the world record for the mile. As founder and president of Jim Ryun Sports, Inc., he is also involved in a number of marketing and public relations campaigns connected to sport. He has four children and two grandchildren and lives on a farm in rural Kansas.

**Steve Scott** is the current American-record holder in the mile, and the men's and women's cross-country and track coach at California State University, San Marcos. He won a silver medal in the 1500 meters at the 1983 world championships, and he holds the record for most sub-four-minute miles run, 137.

**Peter Snell** calls Dallas, Texas, home, where he is an associate professor of cardiology at the Southwestern Medical Center. He is an avid orienteerer, and was recently selected as New Zealand's greatest athlete of the 20th century in recognition of his two Olympic 800-meter gold medals (1960, 1964), his Olympic 1500-meter gold medal (1964), and his three-year reign as mile world-record holder.

**William Tanui** is in the twilight of his career after consistently holding a top place in the end-of-year rankings for both the mile and the 800 meters for close to a decade. The 1992 Olympic 800-meter champion, Tanui lives in Kenya where he continues to train as well as coach young runners. He is also interested in organizing a mile race in Nairobi in hopes of producing Kenya's first ever-sub-four-minute mile.

**Pekka Vasala**, the 1972 Olympic 1500-meter champion, is the managing director of Finland's largest sport and fitness facility, Vierumäki, located in Lahti, just north of Helsinki. He serves on the Finnish Olympic Committee and is involved with the running career of his son, who has current bests of 1:49 for 800 meters and 3:44 for 1500 meters.

**John Walker** owns and operates an equestrian tack shop in Manurewa, Auckland. He set the mile world record in 1975 and won the Olympic 1500 meter title in 1976. He is a local city counselor and involved in numerous charities and public causes. He remains healthy and strong as he works every day to manage his Parkinson's disease.

**Dan Wilson** is a recent graduate of the University of Connecticut, and is currently pursuing his running ambitions full time in Blowing Rock, North Carolina.

## Mile World Record Progression

| | | | |
|---|---|---|---|
| **John Paul Jones** (United States) | 4:14.4 | May 31, 1913 | Cambridge, MA, USA |
| **Norman Taber** (United States) | 4:12.6 | July 16, 1915 | Cambridge, MA, USA |
| **Paavo Nurmi** (Finland) | 4:10.4 | August 23, 1923 | Stockholm |
| **Jules Ladoumegue** (France) | 4:09.2 | Oct 10, 1931 | Paris |
| **Jack Lovelock** (New Zealand) | 4:07.6 | July 15, 1933 | Princeton, NJ, USA |
| **Glenn Cunningham** (United States) | 4:06.8 | June 16, 1934 | Princeton, NJ, USA |
| **Sydney Wooderson** (U.K.) | 4:06.4 | Aug 28, 1937 | Motspur Park, England |
| **Gunder Hägg** (Sweden) | 4:06.2 | July 1, 1942 | Göteborg, Sweden |
| **Arne Andersson** (Sweden) | 4:06.2 | July 10, 1942 | Stockholm |
| **Gunder Hägg** | 4:04.6 | Sept 4, 1942 | Stockholm |
| **Arne Andersson** | 4:02.6 | July 1, 1943 | Göteborg, Sweden |
| **Arne Andersson** | 4:01.6 | July 18, 1944 | Malmö, Sweden |
| **Gunder Hägg** | 4:01.4 | July 17, 1945 | Malmö, Sweden |
| **Roger Bannister** (United Kingdom) | 3:59.4 | May 6, 1954 | Oxford, England |
| **John Landy** (Australia) | 3:58.0 | June 21, 1954 | Turku, Finland |
| **Derek Ibbotson** (United Kingdom) | 3:57.2 | July 19, 1957 | London, England |
| **Herb Elliott** (Australia) | 3:54.5 | Aug 6, 1958 | Dublin, Ireland |
| **Peter Snell** (New Zealand) | 3:54.4 | Jan 27, 1962 | Wanganui, NZ |
| **Peter Snell** (New Zealand) | 3:54.1 | Nov 17,1964 | Auckland, NZ |
| **Michel Jazy** (France) | 3:53.6 | June 9, 1965 | Rennes, France |
| **Jim Ryun** (United States) | 3:51.3 | July 17, 1966 | Berkeley, CA, USA |
| **Jim Ryun** (United States) | 3:51.1 | June 23,1967 | Bakersfield, CA, USA |
| **Filbert Bayi** (Tanzania) | 3:51.0 | May 17,1975 | Kingston, Jamaica |
| **John Walker** (New Zealand) | 3:49.4 | Aug 12, 1975 | Göteborg, Sweden |
| **Sebastian Coe** (United Kingdom) | 3:48.95 | July 17, 1979 | Oslo |
| **Steve Ovett** (United Kingdom) | 3:48.8 | July 1, 1980 | Oslo |
| **Sebastian Coe** (United Kingdom) | 3:48.53 | Aug 19, 1981 | Zurich, Switzerland |
| **Steve Ovett** (United Kingdom) | 3:48.40 | Aug 26, 1981 | Koblenz, Germany |
| **Sebastian Coe** (United Kingdom) | 3:47.33 | Aug 28, 1981 | Brussels, Belgium |
| **Steve Cram** (United Kingdom) | 3:46.31 | July 27, 1985 | Oslo |
| **Noureddine Morceli** (Algeria) | 3:44.39 | Sept 5, 1993 | Rieti, Italy |
| **Hicham El Guerrouj** (Morocco) | 3:43.13 | July 7, 1999 | Rome |

## New Sub-4-Milers by Year Beginning in 1954

| | | | | | | | | | |
|---|---|---|---|---|---|---|---|---|---|
| 1954 | 2 | 1964 | 12 | 1974 | 25 | 1984 | 28 | 1994 | 29 |
| 1955 | 3 | 1965 | 12 | 1975 | 19 | 1985 | 29 | 1995 | 24 |
| 1956 | 5 | 1966 | 12 | 1976 | 13 | 1986 | 26 | 1996 | 28 |
| 1957 | 7 | 1967 | 12 | 1977 | 28 | 1987 | 24 | 1997 | 30 |
| 1958 | 4 | 1968 | 10 | 1978 | 20 | 1988 | 30 | 1998 | 34 |
| 1959 | 1 | 1969 | 10 | 1979 | 26 | 1989 | 22 | 1999 | 24 |
| 1960 | 4 | 1970 | 12 | 1980 | 26 | 1990 | 24 | 2000 | 27 |
| 1961 | 0 | 1971 | 18 | 1981 | 23 | 1991 | 40 | 2001 | 30 |
| 1962 | 12 | 1972 | 14 | 1982 | 32 | 1992 | 22 | 2002 | 18 |
| 1963 | 5 | 1973 | 22 | 1983 | 36 | 1993 | 25 | | |

# Nations' First Sub-4-Miler

| | | | |
|---|---|---|---|
| Algeria | Amar Brahmia | 3:57.20 | Sept 9, 1981 |
| Australia | John Landy | 3:58.0 | June 21, 1954 |
| Austria | Dietmar Millonig | 3:57.7 | June 13, 1979 |
| Belarus | Azat Rakipov | 3:57.88 | July 26, 1994 |
| Belgium | Roger Moens | 3:58.9 | Sept 4, 1957 |
| Brazil | Joaquim Cruz | 3:53.00 | May 13, 1984 |
| Burundi | Vénuste Niyongabo | 3:54.71 | Sept 3, 1993 |
| Canada | Dave Bailey | 3:59.1 | June 11, 1966 |
| Colombia | Jacinto Navarette | 3:59.87 | Feb 13, 1987 |
| Croatia | Branko Zorko | 3:59.45 | May 22, 1993 |
| Cuba | Luis Medina | 3:58.1 | May 11, 1979 |
| Czechoslovakia | Stanislav Jungwirth | 3:59.1 | July 19, 1957 |
| Denmark | Gunnar Nielsen | 3:59.1 | June 1, 1956 |
| Dominica | Steve Agar | 3:57.37 | May 11, 1997 |
| Ethiopia | Seyoume Negatu | 3:59.81 | June 7, 1981 |
| Finland | Olavi Vuorisalo | 3:59.1 | Aug 7, 1957 |
| France | Michel Jazy | 3:59.8 | Oct 3, 1962 |
| Germany | Siegfried Valentin | 3:56.5 | May 28, 1959 |
| Greece | Spyros Hristopoulos | 3:56.11 | May 30, 1992 |
| Holland | Haico Scharn | 3:59.3 | Sept 4, 1973 |
| Hungary | László Tábori | 3:59.0 | May 28, 1955 |
| Iceland | Jon Didriksson | 3:57.63 | Aug 25, 1982 |
| Italy | Francesco Arese | 3:57.8 | Oct 9, 1969 |
| Ireland | Ron Delany | 3:59.0 | June 1, 1956 |
| Jamaica | Byron Dyce | 3:59.6 | May 16, 1971 |
| Japan | Takashi Ishii | 3:59.7 | Dec 10, 1977 |
| Kenya | Kipchoge Keino | 3:54.16 | Aug 30, 1965 |
| Kuwait | Bashar Ibrahim | 3:59.84 | Mar 10, 2001 |
| Luxembourg | Justin Gloden | 3:59.9 | Aug 17, 1980 |
| Mexico | Juan Martínez | 3:58.4 | May 24, 1975 |
| Morocco | Said Aouita | 3:57.75 | Aug 20, 1982 |
| New Zealand | Murray Halberg | 3:57.5 | Aug 6, 1958 |
| Norway | Arne Kvalheim | 3:59.4 | May 6, 1967 |
| Poland | Zbigniew Orywal | 3:58.6 | Sept 3, 1958 |
| Portugal | Fernando Mamede | 3:59.43 | Aug 6, 1976 |
| Qatar | Ahmed Warsama | 3:59.74 | Aug 31, 1991 |
| Rhodesia | Terry Sullivan | 3:59.8 | Sept 23, 1960 |
| Romania | Oliviu Olteanu | 3:58.18 | May 29, 1994 |
| Russia | Valeriy Toropov | 3:58.92 | Aug 17, 1979 |
| Rwanda | Alexis Sharangabo | 3:57.82 | Aug 19, 2000 |
| Senegal | Moussa Fall | 3:59.44 | Aug 6, 1986 |
| Slovakia | Róbert Stefko | 3:58.20 | July 7, 1998 |
| Slovenia | Bekim Bahtiri | 3:58.89 | Aug 25, 1993 |
| Somalia | Jama Aden | 3:56.82 | July 19, 1983 |
| South Africa | DeVilliers Lamprecht | 3:59.7 | Nov 13, 1964 |
| Spain | Alberto Estebán | 3:59.2 | July 2, 1968 |
| Sudan | Omer Khalifa | 3:56.96 | Sept 9, 1979 |
| Sweden | Dan Waern | 3:59.3 | July 19, 1957 |
| Switzerland | Rolf Gysin | 3:56.88 | Aug 16, 1974 |
| Tanzania | Filbert Bayi | 3:52.86 | July 2, 1973 |
| Tunisia | Fethi Baccouche | 3:57.90 | June 11, 1987 |
| Ukraine | Andrey Bulkovskiy | 3:55.28 | Aug 17, 1994 |
| Uganda | Julius Achon | 3:59.53 | Jan 27, 1996 |
| United Kingdom | Roger Bannister | 3:59.4 | May 6, 1954 |
| United States | Don Bowden | 3:58.7 | June 1, 1957 |
| Yugoslavia | Bosko Bozinovic | 3:59.6 | June 13, 1979 |
| Zimbabwe | Phillimon Hanneck | 3:58.81 | Feb 15, 1992 |

Photo courtesy of Mike Barnow

Originally from New York, Jim Denison currently lives and works in England. His features on running appear regularly in *Athletics Weekly* and *Running Fitness*. Additionally, he teaches sports writing at De Montfort University. Still an active runner, Denison attended Fordham University in the mid-1980s on a track scholarship and went on to post best times of 4:07 for the mile and 3:44 for 1500 meters. He later studied sport sociology and creative writing at the University of Illinois, earning a Ph.D. in 1994. He lives with his wife, the scholar and dancer, Pirkko Markula, in their home in Exeter.

To contact the author: j_denison@hotmail.com